D1269390

The Story of Money

THE STORY OF
MONEY

by A. H. Quiggin

Frontispiece and coins by
EVETTE SUMMERS
Other illustrations by
DAPHNE KENNETT

ROY PUBLISHERS NEW YORK

Printed in Great Britain

Contents

Money making about A.D. 1500.

INTRODUCTION

This is an attempt to tell the story of money, how, why, when, where and by what people it was first used, and what forms it took before the invention of coins.

It will be useful to start by seeing what we mean by money, and it is surprising to find that a word in such common use is so difficult to define. For practical purposes, money means something that someone will give or take in return for goods or services, thus acting as a *medium of exchange*. Money must also be a *standard of value* by which goods and services can be estimated, so that a fair exchange can be made to satisfy giver and receiver. And it must also serve as a *store of wealth*, a means by which a man can amass riches.

Anything commonly accepted as a medium of exchange, a standard of value and a store of wealth can claim to be called money, and scores of strange articles are or have been used as money in various parts of the world, starting in early times when cattle or lumps of silver and gold were "money" to the use of cigarettes as "money" in prisons.

It is not easy to see why some articles have become money and not others, but there are certain qualities which have influenced the choice as we can prove by our own experience. We feel that money should be easy to handle and to carry; it should be of some material which will stand handling without getting worn out; it should be of different materials, weights or sizes so that it can be exchanged for things of high or low value; it should be easily recognised and have its value marked on it to show that it is genuine.

In brief, money should be *portable*, *durable*, *divisible* and *distinguishable*. But it is more important that it should be *something that everybody wants*.

Few examples of primitive money pass all these tests, but by seeing how and why they developed and how they were used, we can trace the story of money from the earliest times down to the present use of coins all over the civilised world.

Note on Frontispiece:—To the left we see the furnace, with crucibles containing the precious metals. Beside it sits the mint master at his desk, his balance by his side. In the centre sits a workman with his anvil embedded in a tree trunk, hammering a sheet of metal to flatten it to the right thickness. To the left the man cuts the sheet into blanks, shaping them with his scissors. To the right the boy hands these blanks to the man who, striking them between dies, makes them into coins. (With acknowledgements to Messrs. Spink and Peter Seaby.)

PEOPLE WITHOUT MONEY

The prudent British housewife, before going to market, makes sure that she has money in her purse. And the money will be either in coins or in paper notes. It is difficult for us to realise that there are markets all over the world where the buying and selling of goods is the chief business of everyone, but where money, as we understand it, would be no use at all. A handful of shells, a few beads, a lump or bar of iron, a plaited mat, or some dogs' teeth (*1*) might be useful for exchanges, but shillings and pence, even a golden sovereign, would buy nothing.

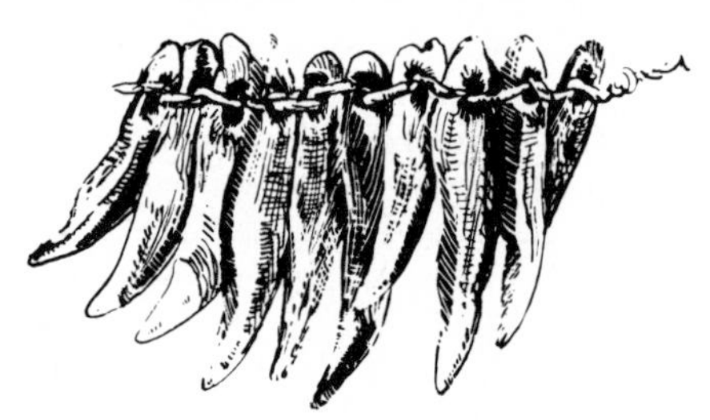

1. Dogs' teeth, New Britain.

In many out-of-the-way parts of the world there is no money because there is no need for it. Throughout great regions of Africa, among the native tribes of North and South America, the Australian aborigines and the islanders of the Pacific, buying and selling are still mainly a matter of barter. So much salt is exchanged for potatoes or so much grain for fish. An Eskimo might bring a silver-fox skin to the store and get in exchange some flour, tobacco, sugar, matches or other luxuries. A native of Borneo, wanting a piece of cloth, would hunt in the jungle for bees' nests until he had collected a lump of beeswax which he would take to the bazaar to get what he wanted. A man in New Guinea collects sago and exchanges it for a cooking pot. An Australian might trade a kangaroo or wallaby skin for a bit of iron to make a spear head. This barter is very much like the swapping that goes on at school when knives and pencils, foreign stamps and white mice are exchanged without the use of money.

ANCIENT EGYPT

It is not only in out-of-the-way parts of the world nor only among backward peoples that moneyless societies can be discovered. Egypt, with its lively trade and even a system of banking, had no coinage until the fourth century B.C. Rameses III, one of the richest of the Pharaohs, who reigned more than a thousand years before our era, had wealth in the shape of cattle and grain, silver and gold, the gold being in the form of solid bars or rings, or bags of gold dust. We

2. Weighing gold rings, Ancient Egypt.

3. Market scene, Ancient Egypt.

can see in an Egyptian wall painting (*2*), gold rings being weighed in a balance against weights in the shapes of animals.

But the ordinary people traded by barter. Once or twice a year, the sleepy Egyptian towns woke up for their religious festivals which attracted crowds from far and near by boat or by caravan, to honour the local god and to trade. The country folk brought their cattle, their grain and their vegetables, the hunters their game and the fishermen their fish, while carpenters, smiths, jewellers, potters, leather-makers and small traders all displayed their goods in the market. Tools, shoes, mats, pots of ointment, necklaces and rings were haggled over and there are records of honey, beds, sticks, oil, pickaxes and clothes exchanged for a bull or a she-ass. A wall painting from a tomb at Saqqara (*3*) illustrates a market scene. One man is offering a necklace in exchange for onions and corn. Another wants a small bottle of oil in place of a pair of sandals, but the seller demands a string of cowries. A couple are arguing about the exchange of a fan and some fish hooks. Silver and gold would rarely be seen, and if metal was used it was in the form of copper wire, usually bent for convenience and weighed for each transaction.

CHINA

China gives us another example of a country which, in its early days was self-sufficient and independent of outside trade, and even trade within the empire was discouraged, traders ranking far below farmers in the social scale. The family was the unit and the family was to a large extent self-supporting, each member rendering services in return for lodging, food and clothing. Gold and silver were less precious than jade, and though bronze coins (*4*) come early in Chinese history, their value was so variable that people often preferred the certainty of bartering goods for goods, and at times coins disappeared altogether. The story of the evolution of money in China is described later (pp. 29–32).

INCA, PERU

One more moneyless society of early days may be considered here, that of Peru under the rule of the Inca. When the Spaniards arrived in Peru in the sixteenth century they found there a communistic system which might be described as a 'welfare state'. Every able-bodied man or woman (with certain exceptions) had an appointed task in agriculture, herding or industry. Even the blind, the crippled and the small children were given work on the roads, guarding the herds of llama and alpaca, scaring the birds from the maize crops or sorting cotton seeds. All this labour was strictly supervised. There were overseers, sometimes as many as one to every five families, who made out the time tables, organised the work and collected the produce in grain, meat, fleeces, metal-work, pottery, cloth, etc., which all belonged to the state. The state in return provided land, lodging, food, clothing and raw materials for all the workers. No man could change his occupation or leave his village, he could not marry without permission or even cut his hair except in the prescribed fashion accorded to his rank. The magnificence of the Inca court and palaces, where the utensils were of gold and silver, the splendidly engineered roads with frequent rest houses, the elaborate system of rapid communication, the hundreds of miles of aqueducts, terraces and irrigation channels all indicate a highly organised society. But there was no trade and there was no money. The Peruvian state has been compared to that of a beehive, well organised and efficient, buzzing with activity but with no individuality and no freedom.

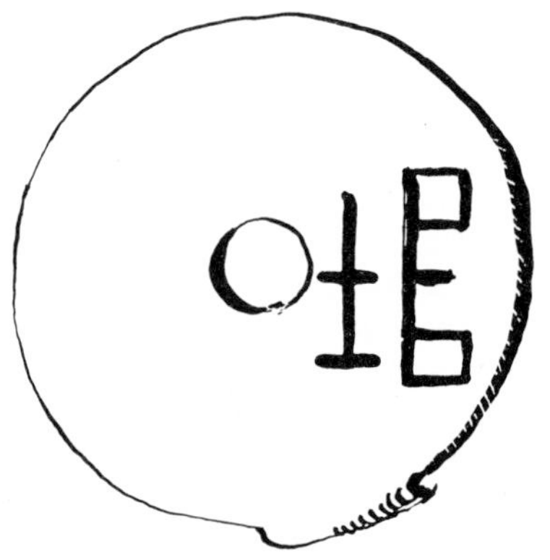

4. Heavenly coin, China.

MONASTERIES AND MANORS

In Europe we may take the monastery in the Middle Ages as an example of a society in which money played little or no part because it was not needed. The monks rendered services in return for housing, food and clothing; each had his task and the result of their common labour was shared by all. The group was practically self-supporting and self-sufficient, and money, though freely used in the world outside the monastery, was rarely seen within its walls.

Nor was money more necessary in the medieval manor, for there also its place was taken by services rendered. The peasants supplied grain, cattle, milk, cheese, vegetables and other foodstuffs, the miller provided the flour, while smiths, carpenters and other workers gave their services in place of rent, rates and taxes, or in exchange for other goods.

Money plays such a large part in our daily lives that it is difficult to picture life without it. Yet this importance has grown up only in the last few centuries. It is calculated that in the thirteenth century, at the beginning of the reign of Edward I, all the coins in the British Isles would have added up to only some £400,000, and not above £1 million before the Spanish discoveries of gold and silver in America in the sixteenth century, looted and brought back by British privateers to supply the mint.

MODERN MONEYLESS SOCIETIES

People who live by collecting food provided by nature, such as wild animals, birds, fish, wild vegetables, seeds, birds' eggs, honey, etc., can be entirely independent of money or even of barter. They may be islanders with no near neighbours with whom to trade, who therefore have to live on whatever their islands can provide and have to develop a self-sufficiency which is made easier by the "double-larder" of sea and land.

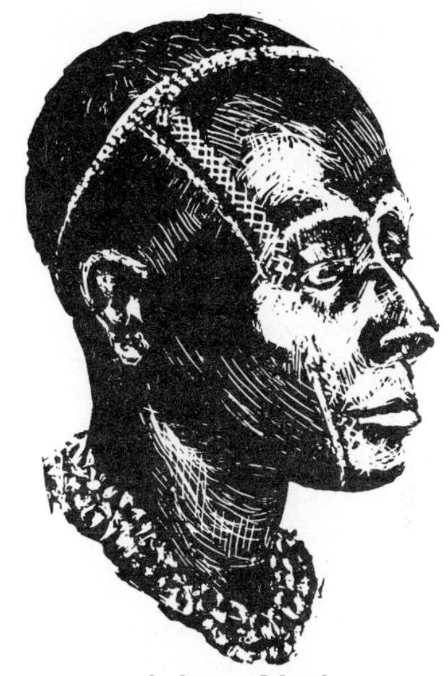

5. Andaman Islander.

The Negrito inhabitants of the Andaman Islands some 700 miles off the coast of Bengal were until lately entirely isolated and entirely self-supporting. Pigs, yams, various fruits and honey were collected on land, dugong, turtle, fish, crabs, etc., from the sea and sea-shore, enough for all. The inland folk had supplies of white clay and red earth, while the folk living by the shores collected *dentalium* and other shells. Coloured earth and shells were effective decoration as the illustration (5) shows, and these were exchanged as presents on the special occasions when there were meetings. But they were never bartered. Presents were merely an expression of good will, and though of course the giver expected an expression of good will in return, the present-giving rarely had any economic advantage on either side.

When plantations of rubber and coconut were started after the closure of the convict station in 1921, money, hitherto unknown, was introduced for paying wages.

PRESENT-GIVING AND GIFT-EXCHANGE

It is easy to see how the custom of present-giving or gift-exchange would lead to the invention and use of money. Certain gifts in common use, such as shells, knives or hoes, mats or baskets, became conventional, thus increasing and steadying their value. They could then be used in exchange for other goods. In New Zealand, for example, present-giving was an important ceremony before the coming of the white voyagers, as it was also in Fiji; it accompanied the trade among the natives of New Guinea and Torres Straits, and it was a complicated social custom, which often led to bankruptcy among the tribes of the north-west coast of North America.

The object of present-giving in New Zealand, as among the Andaman Islanders, was to show good will and to encourage friendly relations. Food, clothing (made of native flax), stone weapons and ornaments all had their exchange value, and though there was no bargaining—that would have been regarded as most improper—anyone who received a present was bound to maintain his reputation for generosity by giving back an equivalent, or to increase it by returning more than he received. When white traders came from overseas, they started to barter, offering trade goods, and even money, in exchange for local products. It was a common custom for the natives to place hundreds of baskets of potatoes in a row on the shore, and the traders would put a stick of tobacco and a farthing on each basket, an exchange which gave satisfaction to all. Here we can see how sudden was the jump from a moneyless people to a money-using community.

The Fijian *solevu* or Great Presentation was not regarded as barter, though here the exchange was of definite economic value. One tribe owned salt pans. Another had clay pits and made pots. Another specialised in making mats, in carving bowls or making canoes. The *solevu* was the formal presentation from one group to another. For example the salt-owning people would send a message to say that they wished to bring a present of salt to the people who made the mats. The mat-makers accepted and the salt was ceremonially handed over with other presents. Both sides kept accurate memories of the value of the presents and in course of time the mat-makers would propose a return *solevu* and hand over the equivalent of the value of salt in mats. If there was too much time-lag, or if the mats were considered a poor return, nothing would be said, the ceremony would not be spoilt by any complaints, but rumours might be heard, hints might be dropped, perhaps even jeering songs might be sung and reputations would be in jeopardy until the number of mats gave satisfaction.

Here also the trader from outside upset local customs, and salt, mats, pots, bowls and canoes were exchanged for trade goods and for coined money.

6. Copper, North America.

The *potlatch* (the word means "gift") of the north-west coast of America was an intricate form of present-giving quite distinct from barter. It was a means by which a man or a tribe could acquire influence and prestige, and lay up stores for future distribution. Birthdays, name days, betrothals, weddings and many other ceremonial events were celebrated by present-giving on a huge scale. Skins, horses, blankets, guns and the famous *coppers* (*6*) were all distributed, exchanged or loaned (at high interest) and, as elsewhere, gifts of equal or higher value were expected in return. The greatest distinction and prestige was attained by the man who could afford not only to give, but to destroy property as evidence of his wealth and power. The coppers are sheets of metal some two or three feet high, beaten out into conventional shapes rather like shields, usually engraved with the animal crest of the owner. Some were valued at several thousand blankets and the man who could "break a copper" was great indeed. The reckless rivalry of the potlatch and the bankruptcy that was often the result of it led to its prohibition by the Canadian Government.

The widely-spread custom of present-giving or gift-exchange must not be overlooked in the story of money as it prepares the way for barter, and barter is among the most important, though not the only influence at work in the evolution of money.

BARTER AND "SILENT TRADE"

Barter develops all over the world wherever some people have goods that others want, and especially in those parts where Nature has distributed her gifts unevenly. We can trace this even in Britain and as long ago as the Stone Age. Flint only occurs in chalk districts, so in the days when flint was more precious than gold, the best kind from Grimes Graves on the borders of Norfolk, or from Cissbury on the South Downs, was traded along the trackways, though we have no evidence of what was given in return.

Sometimes the barter was in the form of *silent trade*, so called because the traders never met. Herodotus described silent trade along the west coast of Africa some five centuries B.C. and it can still be seen in Africa at the present day.

The little pygmies of the central forested area live by hunting game, and they exchange this with the negroes on the edge of the forest who grow vegetables and grain. But they do not meet. When the pygmy has had a successful hunt and eaten as much as he possibly can, he waits until it is dark and then takes what he has left to the entrance of the village. He hangs it on a branch or skewers it to the trunk of a tree. In the morning the villagers take the meat and leave maize, manioc or yams in return. They are careful to give honest value, for the little folk who will come the next evening to fetch their due are not to be tricked, and they have a habit of showing resentment with poisoned arrows.

Another example comes from Northern Rhodesia. On the borders of the Lukanga swamp the natives grow millet and maize and they are glad to have fish to vary the monotony of the daily meal of porridge. They take some grain and leave it at the edge of the swamp and light a fire as a signal. The fisher folk come by night, carry off the grain and leave dried fish in its place.

Barter reaches its highest pitch in African markets off the beaten track of civilised trade. It is a sort of game into which men and women fling themselves with enthusiasm. It is an outlet for their highest enjoyment in voluble argument and excited gesticulation. A stranger is appalled by the noise and sickened by the heat and crowds and fearful that at any moment the fierce arguments may break out into personal violence and riot, but for many it is the chief entertainment of the week. The seller is bound to overestimate his wares just as the buyer is bound to undervalue them, and so the bargaining continues. A man will exchange and re-exchange his goods over and over again in the market, and return home after his day's work without any financial gain, yet feeling that the day has been well spent. No wonder that he prefers direct barter of goods for goods, or the varying values of local currencies to the fixed money and prices ordained by Government which sadly limit his entertainment.

INCONVENIENCE OF BARTER

It is a popular belief that the use of money was evolved from the custom of barter, which develops from everyman's wish to get something he hasn't got, in exchange for something he has. But it does not seem to be quite as simple as that, for we do not find the moneyless people worried by the inconvenience of barter, nor favourite articles of barter developing naturally into money. To us, the inconvenience of barter is very evident but it does not seem to trouble the primitive trader, who often prefers barter, even where money is known and used, as it gives him increased opportunities of profit.

The inconvenience of barter from the native point of view is illustrated in the picture of the Dyak of Borneo, wandering for days in the bazaar with his lump of beeswax which he has collected in the jungle, unable to find anyone who will take it in exchange for the particular cloth or whatever it is he wants. He has no idea of selling his beeswax and then buying the cloth. He collected the wax for the one particular object, time is of no consequence and no doubt in the end he is satisfied.

The inconvenience of barter from the civilised point of view is very different and many examples of exasperation

7. Woman with Cowries.

might be quoted. Take the case of Lieut. Cameron, sent out to the aid of Livingstone in 1873. He started from the coast with the usual trade goods, paying his way with trade beads. But after crossing Lake Tanganyika beads were no use. He had to exchange them for copper crosses (*15*). Farther on copper crosses were rejected, and nothing was acceptable but slaves, goats or cowries (*33*). Here he was delayed for weeks trying to collect enough cowries at exorbitant rates to pay for a canoe to continue on his journey. But even when he had collected twice as many cowries as a canoe was worth, the chief would not sell. Cowries were all very well for small purchases, but he didn't want such masses of them. In fact, he explained, the transaction would be a dead loss. His wives would grab all the cowries for personal ornament (*7*) and he would not be any the better fed or served. Slaves and goats were a far better investment, they bred and increased and repaid his outlay while the cowries remained just cowries.

We need not travel to Africa to see the inconvenience of barter. It could have been seen in England rather more than a century ago. Factory workers used to be paid in goods in place of money and here is one man's experience. "When Saturday night came I had to turn out with a certain quantity of meat and candles or tobacco or ale or whatever I had drawn in wages to dispose of at a serious loss. I used to take a can of ale to the barber to get shaved with and a can of ale to the sweep to sweep my chimney. I used to take my beef, at 7d. a lb., and sell it to the coal woman that I had my coal from, for 5d., and any bit of sugar or tea or anything of the kind, I used to get from the grocer by swapping soap or starch."

All such inconveniences from which English workmen suffered before the final amendment of the Truck Act in 1887 are avoided in simpler societies by various systems of credit, by payments in services, or by deferred payment and long-standing debts that descend from generation to generation, without evolving money in the process. We find very few examples of money developing locally to supply local wants. Money is commonly introduced by travellers and traders from outside.

BRIDE-PRICE AND BLOOD-MONEY

When local objects of barter develop

into local money (and a few of these persist even to the present day in spite of the introduction of coins), these survivals appear to be derived less from the custom of barter than from two far older customs, marriage and murder.

For acquiring a wife or for killing a man some payment must be made or some equivalent must be given. Among the less advanced societies, as formerly in our own, a young man wanting to marry has to collect a contribution to present to his prospective father-in-law, who, in a community where women do most of the work, suffers substantially in losing the services of his daughter. The custom is called *bride-price* or *bride-wealth* because no better term has been discovered, but it is a matter of marriage settlement rather than of sale and purchase.

In the same way the killing of a man or woman means the loss of services to family or group and this must be compensated by payments. If native law does not demand a life for a life it usually insists on something substantial in its place.

Here we see the reason for amassing a *store of wealth*, the necessity for calculating a *standard of value* and the material for a *means of exchange*, i.e., the birth of the idea of money.

TRIBUTE OR TAXES

Besides its importance in acquiring wives and compensating for killings, one other influence in the evolution of money must be added here, the influence of tribute or taxation. Contributions more or less voluntary by tribesmen to their chiefs or conquerors were the earliest forms of taxation. It was obviously an advantage if the contributions were portable and divisible, and still more advantageous if they could be amassed and form a store of wealth. Here again are the chief qualities that we have seen are needed for money.

MONEY-SUBSTITUTES: CATTLE

"Bride-price", "blood-price", tribute and taxes all demand payments and so play their part, with barter, in the evolution of money. What forms did these payments take before the invention of coins?

The list of money-substitutes is a long one, with more than a hundred items collected from all over the world. We will choose some of the more important and more generally used, such as cattle, grain, salt and metal objects which people are still using or were using until recently in out-of-the-world regions, in place of coins.

Throughout a great part of the Old World, wealth in early days consisted in *cattle*. From Ireland in the west, across Europe to India and Mongolia and Indo-China in the east, and from Iceland and Scandinavia in the north, to north, east and southernmost Africa, a man's wealth was calculated in his flocks and herds and the value of his goods was described in terms of cattle. In this connection cattle must be understood to include not only oxen and cows, buffalo and their kin, but also horses and mares, reindeer, camels, sheep, goats and pigs, and, it may be added, slaves as well.

Throughout this vast region, cattle were a store of wealth, a standard of value, and often a medium of exchange, three of the main uses of money. So if only cattle were portable, durable, divi-

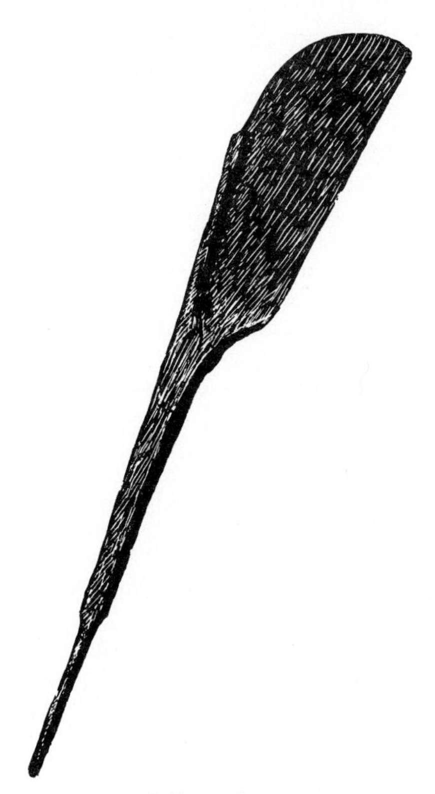

8. Dao, Assam.

sible and distinguishable with the stamp of authority, it would be difficult not to allow their claim to be called money. Cattle were indisputably one of the first and most wide-spread money-substitutes.

Abraham is described as being very rich in cattle, silver and gold, cattle being mentioned first. The value of a slave in Homer or of a prize in the Greek games was calculated in terms of oxen. The tribute of the King of Leinster (according to the *Annals*, *c.* A.D. 100) was paid in cows, pigs, slaves and cauldrons. In Britain, dowries and fines were paid in cattle and slaves. Even as late as the eighteenth century dowries in Scotland were not in money but in cattle. Dr. Johnson, who travelled in the Western Isles in 1773, says "the lairds do not often give money with their daughters; the question is How many cows a young lady will bring her husband. A rich maiden has from ten to forty; but two cows are a decent fortune for one who pretends to no distinction."

In India (according to the *Laws of Manu*, some six centuries B.C.) a slave girl was worth five cows and a bull. Blood-money, the price for killing a man, might be 1,000 cows and a bull for a high-born victim, down to ten cows and a bull for a commoner. Throughout the hilly parts of Burma and Assam a man's wealth consisted in his live stock, and Government assessed him not in rupees, but in buffalo and pigs, cocks and hens. Buffalo, supplemented by rice, knives (*daos*) (*8*) and gongs were necessary in present-giving, for fines, for "bride-price" or marriage-settlement and for funeral gifts. The accidental killing of a man needed one to ten cows as blood-money according to circumstances.

Illustrations of a cattle-currency or at least of cattle being used as a standard of value can be collected throughout Africa, wherever cattle-rearing is possible, though the reluctance of Africans to part with their beasts discourages their practical use as a medium of exchange.

Among the Nilotic peoples, cattle and wealth are the same thing. In Tanganyika, cows were given for services rendered, though regarded more as gifts than as payments. Goats were the chief

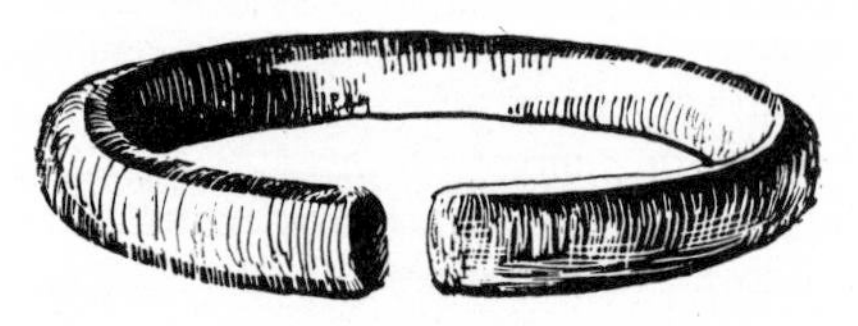

9. Lobolo ring.

evidence of wealth and together with rings (*9*) the chief item in "bride-price" in Portuguese East Africa; oxen formed the average *lobolo*, the bride-money, for the Zulu farther south, and ten head of cattle were the price of a wife in Bechuanaland.

Cows mean wealth, if not money, among the cattle-keeping peoples of Europe, Africa and Asia. Their place is taken in the Melanesian islands by the pig. All the thoughts and cares of the native of the New Hebrides are centred round this, his most precious possession, for his standing in this world and in the next depends on the number and the excellence of his pigs. They are needed in the "purchase" of wives, in ascending the social scale, and in entrance into Paradise.

GRAIN AND SALT

Grain has been used instead of money from the earliest times down to the present day. So we hear of corn in Egypt, barley in Babylonia, millet in the Sudan, maize in Mexico, wheat and rice in India and China, which have been and still are used in place of money. The reasons for the popularity of grain are obvious, for it has most of the characteristics of coins. It is easy to carry in baskets, bags or sacks, it lasts in good condition for at least a season, it can be sorted into large or small quantities, it is universally wanted and though it may vary in quality it can scarcely be imitated.

In Egypt in the fourth century B.C. taxes and rents were collected in grain, mainly wheat, and stored in Government granaries which served as banks (*10*). A man wanting to open an account deposited so much grain. He could thereafter draw upon his deposit by cheque. He could also pay his bills by issuing cheques payable at any of the Government granaries. This system continued long after coinage had been introduced.

10. Ancient Egyptian granary.

The main purpose of grain is, however, to provide food, not wealth, and in spite of its excellence as a money-substitute, its use must be seen rather as a form of barter than as a form of money.

Salt provides a good illustration of an article of barter which in many parts of the world has become a definite medium of exchange, used as we use money. Salt is not found everywhere but it is everywhere wanted, and few people when once they have acquired a taste for salt can do without it.

Wages may have been paid in salt in Rome and the derivation of the word salary from *salarium*, the salt allowance for soldiers, is taken as evidence. Wages are certainly still paid in salt in Africa, where it is universally appreciated. Salt is only found or collected in special areas and as the native foods are usually vegetable, flavourless and monotonous, salt is a prime necessity. And salt is often taken where money is rejected. Road menders in the Congo region are paid in bucketfuls and they spend it, in teaspoonfuls, in the bazaar. Square lumps pass from hand to hand suffering from furtive licks on the way, and though sticky and dirty, still serve as a medium of exchange in the market. In the Niger region in the old slaving days a slave was sold for his weight in salt, though in a time of intertribal war the value of slaves became halved and that of salt doubled. In parts of Nigeria blocks or cakes of salt are still part of the bride-price.

In these examples salt, though used as money, is also a barterable article. It is different however in Abyssinia. There the salt is cut up at the salt mines into blocks of four sizes, valued at a quarter, a half, one, and one and a half dollars, and these were recognised until lately as legal tender for wages and taxes. Salt in blocks serves as money in Morocco also (*11*). In China, in the days of Marco Polo, salt was made into cakes which

11. Salt blocks, North Africa.

were stamped by the state and eighty cakes were equal to a gold bar, though the value increased as they were traded inland.

Salt is certainly an acceptable medium of exchange, the first essential of money, but it fails in some of the characteristics needed for money in its fullest sense. It is not sufficiently durable, being injured by damp and easily broken up; the bars or cakes are not conveniently portable and even though certified by the state the fact that the value always varies with distance from the source of supply limits its general use. That salt is a commodity rather than money is illustrated by the demand for salt in out-of-the-way African villages where coins are refused with the explanation "We cannot eat coins".

METAL CURRENCIES OF AFRICA

Metal objects, including the so-called "tool currencies", provide many examples of barterable goods developing into a medium of exchange, and some of these, losing all barterable value, become merely tokens, with all the characteristics of money.

Iron in lumps and bars, hoops, rings or bangles, knives, spears, hoes, axes and vague and puzzling shapes serve as money throughout much of Africa south of the Sahara, especially where there are no cattle to form the standard of value. Indeed, when a tribe lost all its cattle (as when the Thonga were raided by the Angoni about a century ago), hoes and beads had to take the place of cattle, and instead of the customary ten oxen which were the average *lobolo*, ten hoes were paid as bride-price to the family of the bride.

It is easy to see why iron is so popular in barter. It is everywhere valued for making into tools, weapons or ornaments, so it is everywhere acceptable. It has a scarcity value, as it is not found in all districts, and, where found, is not always worked. Smiths in Africa usually form a separate caste, honoured in some areas, despised in others, and a certain mystery surrounds their craft. Copper is also useful as an easily worked metal, and, being more decorative, makes fashionable ornaments.

Some of these metal objects such as the *manillas* (*12*), bangles or curved bars of the West Coast, the brass rods and hoes (*shoka*) of the Congo region, and the Katanga copper crosses may certainly be called primitive money. They were (many still are) used by the natives in their markets, by traders on the coasts and up the rivers and by travellers and missionaries inland for everyday purchases.

Eight or ten *manillas* were the average price of a male slave at the end of the fifteenth century, but though they were still used as money up to the middle of this century their trading value was only 3d. The copper (later brass) rods, often

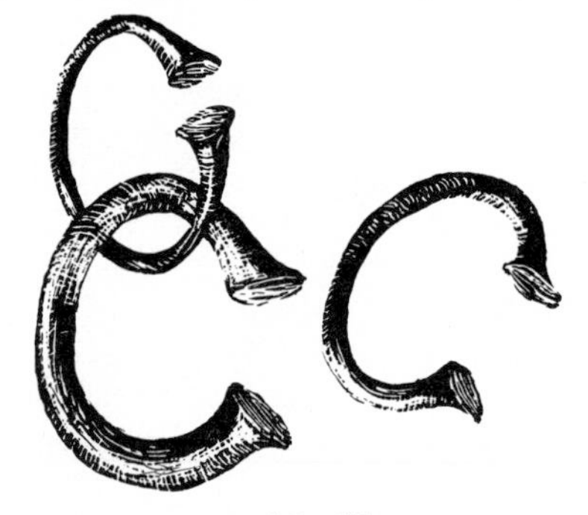

12. Manillas.

13. Mitakos.

made into rings (*mitakos*) (*13*), were the official money of the Congo State and everything was priced in them, though the actual payment might be made in beads, cloth or any other goods. One brass ring would buy an egg, ten a fowl, up to six hundred for a slave and some thousands for an ivory tusk.

The Congo *shokas* are often called hoes, though they look more like truncated spear heads, and although they would be useless either as tool or weapon, they are the only means of buying food and other goods in the market. An average *shoka* would buy three bunches of bananas. The little Yakusu boy (*14*) holds a *shoka* in his right hand and a gigantic spear head, still used in bride-price, in his left.

The copper crosses are also of varying sizes and values. An average cross of about a pound and a half (*15*) would buy five or six fowls (in the Kasai region) ten lengths of cloth or six axes. Slaves, goats, cloth and crosses are demanded in bride-price but especially crosses. Slaves

14. Boy with shoka and spear head, Congo.

15. Copper cross.

and goats may sicken and die, cloth wears out, but copper crosses, immune from such disasters, are the best investment.

Some of these metal currencies have no practical value. They are merely tokens, and, queer though they are, they are used just as we use our coins, though usually only locally and sometimes only within the tribe.

Among the best examples of these local forms of money are the Bubu throwing knives, the Fan "axes", the Kissie pennies and the Nigerian "needle money".

The Fans were one of the most dreaded tribes who invaded the Congo territory. They came originally from the Sudan and they were renowned for their ferocity and for their murderous throwing knives, which could cut off an enemy's leg at twenty yards, and they were used in exchanges and traded for grain. In the western forested area, throwing knives could not be used, but, blunted and unfinished imitations had a trading value, and they were not called knives, but "money" (*16*).

17. Fan axes, West Africa (full size).

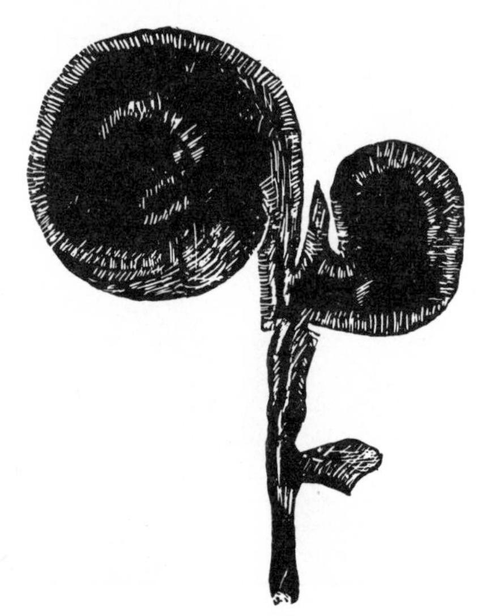

16. Throwing knife, Congo (much reduced).

The Fans themselves, when settled in the Congo region, became collectors of rubber and ivory, and they brought their spoil back to the rich men of the villages, who gave them "axes" in exchange. These are little bundles of light iron rods with splayed ends, bound in threes or in tens (*17*). They are, or were, used solely within the limits of the Fan tribe and their main purpose was for betrothals, when thousands of bundles were paid as bride-price to the father of the bride.

18. Kissie pennies (much reduced).

The so-called *needle money* (*19*) looking like squashed tin-tacks (also called "axe" or "arrow-head money") is queerer still. These little bits of iron, barely half an inch long and so thin that fifty scarcely weigh up to a halfpenny, were money in Southern Nigeria. They are said to have been used in the old days for buying slaves, though, as the exchange value was reckoned at about forty-five to the penny, tens of thousands would have to have been paid for even a cheap slave.

19. Needle money (full size).

Kissie pennies are the currency on the borders of Liberia and Sierra Leone, where they may still be seen in use. They are thin iron rods a foot or more long, flattened out at the ends into "ears" and "feet" (*18*). Two or three will buy a score of oranges, a large bunch of bananas or several kola nuts. The local money-changer, an important character in the market, has a pile of these by his side and he exchanges them at about forty-six to the African shilling. All polite visitors use these "pennies", as it is a compliment to the local chief to use the local money. Here, as with most examples of African primitive money, the chief use is for bride-price. The pennies are tied up into bundles and hundreds of them handed over to the father of the bride.

CHINESE TOOL CURRENCIES

The *tool currencies* of China show how tools in daily use can develop into coins, and the story is a strange one. According to historical records, bronze knives were used as money in China about 1000 B.C. and it is only reasonable to suppose that they represent the knives in common use, blunted and modified to serve as money. The earliest ones are fairly solid and heavy with a ridge round the edge and a large

20. Knife money, China.

21. Spade money, China.

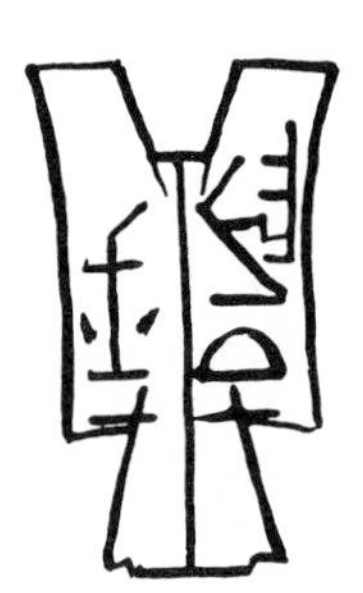

22. Pú, China.

hole in the handle (*20*). They are inscribed, "Knife money", often with the place of origin on one side and the value on the other. In succeeding centuries, the knives become smaller and lighter, weighing barely half an ounce, and the characters are seldom clear. They are found in thousands and there are hundreds of varieties; for each city, each trading centre, and each trading guild had its own mint and issued its own money in the form of knives, spades and other tools.

The knives at first resemble knives. Some of the spade coins look like spades (*21*) and as they are inscribed "knife-coins" or "spade-coins" there is little doubt as to their origin and purpose. But the so-called *pu* coins (*22*) are more puzzling, and this is shown in the translation of the word *pu*, for they have been called hoe, axe, adze, plane, wedge, cloth, shirt or trouser money and this does not exhaust the list. All these "tool coins" were in use perhaps as early as 1000 B.C. and certainly in the centuries following. In a folk song of the sixth century B.C. a girl says to her suitor

"A simple-looking lad you were
Carrying *pu* to exchange for silk
But you came not to purchase silk
You came to make proposals to me."

All the tool coins were abolished by decree about 221 B.C. by the Ch'in Emperor, who attempted to form a uniform currency. But some 200 years later the usurper Wang Mang issued more knife coins, though of a different shape, still less like knives and more like a modern key (*23*). It was at one time

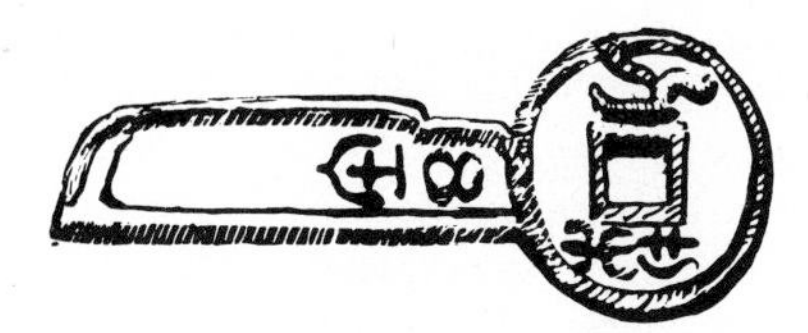

23. Later knife money, China.

believed that these were direct descendants of the earlier knives and that the well-known Chinese *cash* (*40–2*), with square holes, could be traced to the handles of the original knives. But Chinese cash are probably as early in date as the earliest knives, so the sequence of knife to cash is unsupported.

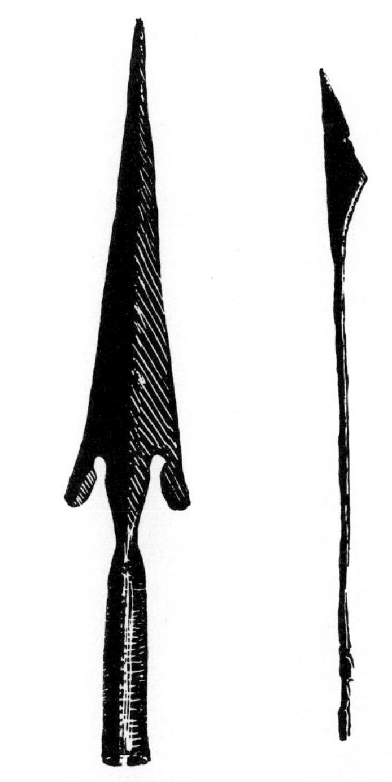

24. Spear head and chabili, Assam.

SOUTH-EAST ASIA

Knives (*daos*), spears (*24*) and hoes are used in Further India in place of money. The hoes and spears are useful, but many of the knives, like the Chinese knives to which they are probably related, are merely tokens. Some, like the Assam *chabili*, are very thin bits of iron splayed out at one end, and serve only as money. They are used in present-giving at feasts, given to the local doctor to avert illness (six for a man and five for a woman) and a bride always carries some to her new home.

In south-east Asia we find silver, copper, tin and alloys used as money, taking different shapes in different parts, such as the *bar money* in Siam (*25*), sometimes scooped out and called *canoe money* (*26*) and the sugar-loaves and "tin hats" of the Malay Peninsula (see p. 29), but their place is now taken by the more convenient round coins.

Out of the hundred and more forms of primitive money used in various parts of

25. Bar money.

26. Canoe money.

the world in the time before coins were made, only a few of the more important can be mentioned here. The more common, cattle, grain, salt and metal objects have been described above. We will confine ourselves to the illustration of three more, used locally in limited areas in the Pacific: the mats of Melanesia, the coconuts of the Nicobar Islands and the "stone money" of Yap in the Caroline Islands.

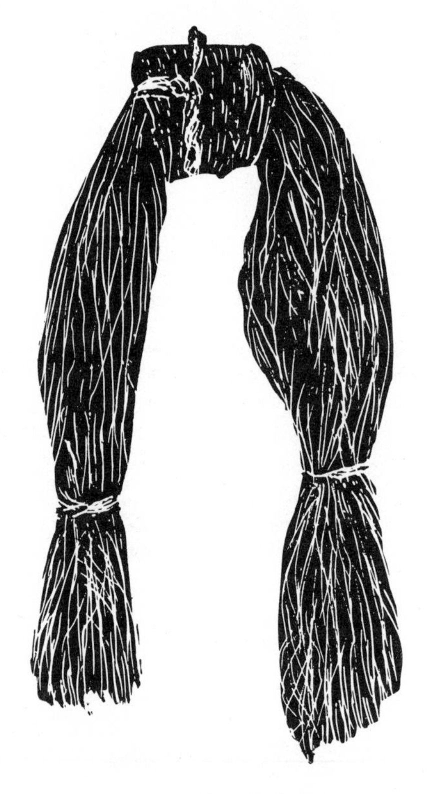

27. Mat, New Hebrides.

MATS AS MONEY

Mats seem to us an unexpected form of money, since they play such an unimportant and humble part in our own lives. But in some of the islands of the Pacific their position is one of importance and dignity. The women plait them from leaf strips and grasses and some of the finer ones are works of art taking years in the making. They are used in present-giving (see p. 6) and they acquire special value when they take part in ceremonies on great occasions. The greatest use is at weddings, for not only do they form the bride-price but the bride's family present mats to the bridegroom. As the women are the mat-makers, the more wives, the more mats, and the more mats a man has, the more wives he can acquire and the higher his position in society. Mats represent wealth and the amassing of them is the ambition of all. Candidates to chieftainship distribute mats to possible supporters. If elected they receive mats from constituents and so increase their stores. We saw that in the New Hebrides pigs were a store of wealth (p. 12). In some of the islands mats are even more important than pigs. Very narrow mats with very long fringes (27) are small change, but more valuable ones represent wealth and the older and more useless, the more value they acquire. These are only used for special payments such as for advancement in secret societies.

COCONUTS AS MONEY

It is easy to see how coconuts could be commonly used in barter, but not so easy to see how they could become money. Coconuts are, however, used as money in

28. Stone money, Yap.

the Nicobar Islands. Rupees and annas are legal tender, but native buyers and sellers prefer coconuts. Everything is bought for coconuts or rather in pairs of coconuts tied together by a bit of the husk. One or two pairs will buy a box of matches or some salt, fish hooks or rice. Some thousands of pairs will buy a gramophone. Canoe racing is one of the most popular sports and canoes are expensive, but they are estimated in coconuts. One island specialises in canoe manufacture and when the natives of another island wanted to buy one they had to pay 35,000 coconuts or the value of 35,000 coconuts. The actual payment was made in pigs and fowls, cloth, spoons and forks and even in rupees and annas, but all was calculated in pairs of coconuts.

THE STONE MONEY OF YAP

Of all the strange forms of primitive money none is stranger than the "stone money" of Yap in the Caroline Islands (*28*). No one knows when or why the idea first started of fetching the white stones looking like millstones, called locally *fae*, from the Pelew Islands some 400 miles away, or from Guam, further still, to serve as money for the islanders of Yap. A group of young men would go out paddling their rafts, day after day over the empty sea, and bring back the stones, the larger the better. The smaller ones, the size of a dinner plate or smaller, are used in the market for buying fish, pigs and vegetables. A lady of rank going shopping would have a file of slaves following each carrying a *fae* on a pole over his shoulder. The larger ones are owned by the village or by wealthy men, whose ambition it is to have an avenue of huge stones (some are ten to twelve feet or more across) leading up to their houses. These stones seem to us an incredibly inconvenient form of money, but they satisfied the Yap islanders as a means of exchange, a standard of value and a store of wealth. Even when, in recent years, German marks or Japanese yen were made compulsory, stones were preferred, and they still retain their value, though American dollars are found handier for ordinary shopping.

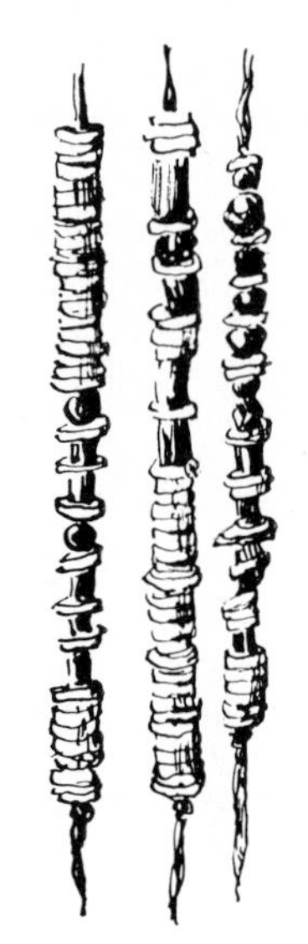

29. Shell money.

SHELL MONEY

To us, used to the convenience of coins, the examples of cattle, salt, grain, hoes or knives, mats, coconuts or mill-stones seem clumsy and unsuitable forms of money, and it is clear that though they may serve their purpose among the less advanced peoples, especially those living in small groups, none of them could become a general currency for trading on a larger scale. Cattle are too cumbersome, grain, salt and coconuts too perishable, tool currencies too awkward. Money to be generally acceptable should be handy, lasting, easy to count and difficult to counterfeit; so far we have met nothing that will pass these tests.

But there is one form of primitive money that more nearly fits in with our ideas of what money should be; this is *shell money*.

In many islands of the Pacific Ocean, from New Guinea and the Admiralties in the north to New Caledonia in the south, and especially in the Solomons group and the Bismarck Archipelago, shell strings are (or were) the ordinary money used in the markets and in trade with other islands (*29*). Money-making here is a laborious process. The men dive for the shells, red, black and white. The women break them up into small pieces, rub them down, drill holes in them and thread them on strings. Then they are ground evenly and serve as decoration and as money. The strings are usually made on the smaller rocky islands where there is little room for gardens and they are exchanged for vegetables from the main-land. Special kinds and special lengths have different values, red being the high-est, perhaps because red shells are scarcer. Often red and white, separated by black (either shells, coconut discs or banana seeds), are strung together. One short string will buy food, taro or yams, ten or twelve fathoms would buy a pig or hire a murderer. It takes 100 lengths, usually measured by the fathom, for a good canoe or a good wife.

Shell money reached its greatest importance in New Britain in the Bismarck Archipelago. Here it was made differently of different shells. Little cowry-like *Nassa* shells were collected from the mangrove branches along the shores, their occupants dried out and the backs of the shells broken, so that they could be forced, rather than threaded, on to a stiff strip

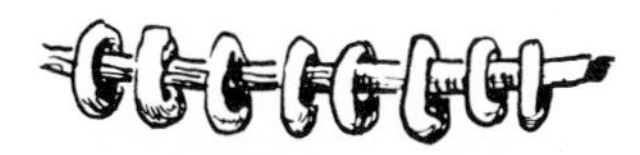

30. Diwarra, New Britain.

of cane (*30*). These strips in fathom lengths formed the money. With this *diwarra* or *tambu* everything could be bought. Anyone going to market would have a short length, often stuck in the hair, and a few shells, easily twisted off, would buy some betel nut, yams or other vegetables, half a fathom would buy a fowl, ten or twenty fathoms (coiled up) would buy a pig, while wives or canoes would run into 100 or 150 fathoms according to quality and market fluctuations. Without it no one could enter a secret society. This cost fifty to sixty fathoms, with greater lengths for advance from grade to grade. For storage, some hundred fathoms were coiled and bound with banana leaves and safely kept in guarded houses. Some of these coils would be as large as cartwheels and would be exhibited from time to time to show the wealth of their owners. The love of this money was the despair of the missionaries. No service, however small, was given without a demand for money, no present without a return. The amassing of coils of *diwarra* was the ambition of all for display during life and still more at death. Shell money here was the medium of exchange, the standard of value and store of wealth, portable, durable, divisible and distinguishable, for it could not be imitated. The German Government prohibited its use by European traders early in the century, but it was still used by the natives, specially for secret societies and bride-price. It is doubtful if any is made now, as it was a slow and laborious process, and natives can earn more in other ways. Its place was taken by sticks of tobacco and German marks, now replaced by Australian shillings.

SHELL MONEY IN AMERICA

Wampum was the name (shortened from the Algonquian *wampumpeag*) for the shell money used by the native Indians of the east coast of America before the Discovery. They collected the white clam shells with purple edges (*Venus mercenaria*) which are fairly common on the Atlantic shores, they cut them into pieces, bored, threaded and ground them down into tubular beads and used the strings for presentations, for peace-making, for bride-price and for blood-price, and for ornaments as well as for money (*31*). The early settlers used wampum strings in trading with the Indians, the value varying with the size and colour of the beads from about three shillings up to ten shillings a fathom. Single beads were from three to six a

31. Wampum (reduced).

penny. Wampum spread across America from east to west and was in common use in fur-trading in the north. Soon the Colonists started making it themselves with steel drills and lathes, the Dutch factories near New York turning out hundreds of strings for Indian trade. It became too common to have any value, and as gin and tobacco were more attractive, it ceased to be used as money.

The shell money on the West Coast of America was different, as the Indians there used *dentalium* (*tusk shells*) found along the shores (*32*). A fathom of these strung on sinew was called *allikochik*, "human beings their shell money", and if of large shells this was the price of a slave. The larger, the more valuable, and men had lines tattooed on the inside of their forearm so that they could easily measure the length. A string of five stretching from the thumbnail to the nearest tattoo mark was worth 25 dollars, but there were few as large as this and a man owning such a string would be renowned far and wide and could provide himself with a high-born wife.

32. Dentalium.

COWRIES

The shell money of the Pacific islands had, as a rule, a limited range, and as, except for *diwarra* (*30*), the strings were not very different from ornaments, the exchanges were often more like barter than money transactions.

There is another form of shell money that had an almost world-wide circulation, from India, China, Siam and Further India in the east, round and across Africa

33. Cowries.

to the west coast, and into America. This was the money *cowry* (*33*).

Cowries have had an adventurous history. They were the money of the trading world for hundreds of years before coins were in general use and they are still used in out-of-the-way parts of their former vast domain. The little shells (*Cypraea moneta*) are found most abundantly in the warm waters of the Indian Ocean, and especially round the Maldive Islands, where they formed the wealth of the royal treasury. Nearly a thousand years ago an Arab historian tells how, when funds were getting low, the sovereign sent out servants to cut branches of coconut palm and throw them into the sea. The little molluscs climbed on to the branches and were collected and spread out on the sand to dry until only the empty shells were left. So the royal bank was filled again. Ships from India brought goods to the Maldives and took back millions of shells packed up in thousands in coconut palm leaves. It was a profitable trade, for even in the seventeenth century we hear of 9,000 or 10,000 cowries being bought for a rupee and sold again for three or four times as much on the mainland of India. Here they were the common small change and found their way into the multiplication table, when eighty cowries went to the *pana*, and sixteen *panas* to the *dramma*. This was a sum in an arithmetic book a thousand years ago:—

"The quarter of a sixteenth of the fifth of three-quarters of two-thirds of a moiety of a *dramma* was given to a beggar by a person from whom he asked alms. Tell me how many cowry shells the miser gave if thou be conversant in arithmetic."

Revenues were paid in cowries in Bengal even in the last century. Fleets of boats were needed to carry them down the rivers, and huge warehouses had to be made to store them, for by 1865 more than 6,000 went to the rupee. Cowries were the currency in China, with ups and downs, and were still in use in Siam in the last century.

Cowries did a brisk trade in Africa. In the fourteenth century, when a million could be bought in the Maldives for a gold *dinar*, they were worth a thousand *dinar* by the time they had travelled along the Arab trade routes and reached Nigeria. In the markets and trading centres of the Sudan an official cowry-counter was appointed to deal with the masses of shells, sorting them by fives into piles of 100 and 1,000. A good cowry-counter could deal with 250,000 or more in a day.

Following the Arabs came the Dutch and Portuguese, the French and the English all trading with cowries round the coasts of Africa and up the rivers. Then came a check. The money cowries, as we have seen, come from the Indian Ocean. But there are cowries (*Cypraea annulus*), often called "ring cowries" from the marking on their backs, on the east coast of Africa. And the merchants found it was more profitable to collect these on the east coast and trade them on the west, without the long journey to the Maldives. At first this was a success, but not for long. Soon the cowries became too common to be of any value, for when 2,000 were worth about sixpence they could be used only for very small purchases.

On the Gold Coast, gold dust was the usual money, weighed by means of peas into *taccoes*, six taccoes making an *ackie*, with sixteen ackies to the ounce. Even a small amount would be tendered by balancing a grain or two on a knife tip, but the commoner small change was in cowries.

In 1869, 16,000 cowries were worth a sovereign, but collecting and counting lessened their value. Some £2,500 worth of cowries from up-country cost £125 for carriage and it took eight men a whole day to count them. When, after 1870, a "head" of cowries, i.e., 2,000, was worth only about eighteen pence they were no longer imported, though they continued in use among the natives for petty transactions.

It is easy to see why cowries were so popular, and we cannot be surprised that they replaced the awkward and clumsy forms of money such as cattle, salt or metal objects which had preceded them in Africa and elsewhere. The shells are attractive in themselves and are much appreciated for ornaments (as we saw on p. 9) and in inland regions they were regarded as charms and amulets with fantastic values. When the first cowries reached Uganda, far from the coast, two shells would buy a woman, but with limitless imports the value fell rapidly and, a generation later, a woman cost 10,000 shells. Off the beaten track farther inland they still had a trading value towards the end of last century; five cowries would buy an egg, and thirty a bunch of bananas. When the rupee was established as legal tender early in the century, 1,000 were reckoned to the rupee, and though strings nominally of a hundred can still be met with, they have mostly disappeared from the markets.

TRADE BEADS

In many parts of Africa cowries held their own as the trading currency until the introduction of coins in recent years. But they had a serious rival in trade beads. These had much the same range as cowries, as they were used by the same traders for native trade. The earliest may have been made in Egypt, where glass blowing was an early invention, and they may have been traded down the West coast of Africa by the Phoenicians some centuries B.C. The *aggry beads* of the Gold Coast (*34*) are traditionally associated with the Phoenicians. Ancient trade beads of similar type have been found in prehistoric hoards in Eastern Asia, in India, and in South and East Africa, indicating an early trade. *Chevron beads* (*35*) of a complicated pattern have been found in prehistoric barrows and Anglo-Saxon graves, on the mainland of Europe and Asia, in the Pacific islands, in Africa and in pre-Columbian graves in North America. Cambay in

34. Aggry beads.

35. Chevron bead.

India and Venice on the Mediterranean were the chief manufacturing centres for beads in historic times, imitated in recent years by factories in Birmingham and in Czechoslovakia—and so skilfully imitated that it needs a microscope to distinguish the modern from the ancient.

So far, the story has been of various objects used as money before the invention or introduction of coins, and many of them are still essential in bride-price. But in ordinary trading none of them could compete with the superior attractions of cowries and beads, iron, cloth and other trade goods, especially gin and tobacco. This makes a complete break in the story of the evolution of money, for while the earlier forms were native products, cowries, beads, iron and trade goods were brought in by foreign traders. Within a generation or two, native money was abandoned and supplanted by foreign coins.

You will notice that most of our examples of money-substitutes have been found in the less advanced parts of the world, and it is not in such regions that we can expect the evolution of money to be illustrated. Such evolution could only take place with favouring circumstances. There must first be suitable metal and skilled metal-workers, with a lively trade, stimulated by well-established trade routes and safe harbours. We may look for these favouring conditions in Asia.

BEGINNINGS OF MONEY IN ASIA

We can see the beginnings of a metal currency in the tin region of the Malay Peninsula. But there, as in Africa, traders from outside with superior coinage supplanted native products. We cannot trace the beginnings of money in India, for we find forms of coinage well established some centuries B.C. and their earlier history is at present uncertain. It seems probable that coins were a local invention in India as in China. In China the whole evolution from primitive to modern money is fully illustrated, though the history is far from simple and the dating is uncertain.

There is a vast difference in the story of money in the Far East from India to the Pacific, when compared with the Near East from India westward to the Mediterranean, though the contrast is due more to politics than to geography. The countries from India eastwards developed more or less independently with only a few links such as trading ports, with the world outside. But the great civilisations of the Nearer East traded with each other and went to war with each other, as each tried to gain dominion over the rest.

ASSYRIA

From the eighth to the seventh century B.C., just before the time when the first coins appear, Assyria was the most powerful state in Western Asia, stretching over the "fertile crescent" from the borders of Persia to the Mediterranean, with Nineveh, "mistress of the world", as its capital. It received tribute in the form of gold and silver, cattle and grain and manufactured goods from allied or conquered peoples including the Ionian Greeks and even the inhabitants of the island of Cyprus. But all this extensive trade was carried on without the use of coins. Daily wages in Assyria were paid in barley. The labourer, usually a slave, could eat what barley he wanted and exchange what was over for other goods. The unit of weight for bargaining was therefore the grain of barley, and 180 grains, roughly a handful, made the shekel, which weighed a little less than a modern English penny. Traders naturally preferred the more convenient lumps of metal, especially silver and bronze, and the first step towards coins was made when the small lumps were made of definite weights and stamped with some device, usually the head of a god. Thus Sennacherib (706–681 B.C.), who destroyed Babylon, rebuilt Nineveh and besieged Jerusalem (II Kings xix), recorded in his annals, "I caused a mould of clay to be set up and bronze to be poured into it to make pieces of half a shekel."

PERSIA

Nineveh fell before the onslaughts of the Medes and Persians in 612 B.C., and Persian coins were the first to circulate throughout the lands of Western Asia, where there was already a network of trade routes to welcome the labour-saving device. Darius, King of Persia, modelled coins on those of Croesus, King of Lydia, and the gold *darics* named after him, but popularly called "Persian archers", were the earliest coins in general use (*47*). When in the following century Alexander the Great conquered the Persians, Greek culture spread throughout his dominions, Greek language, arts and sciences flourished in all the settlements linked by trade with the homeland, and coinage based on Greek models replaced the more primitive forms of money from India in the east to Italy in the west, and later, as we shall see, in Gaul and in Britain.

If we start in the east and travel westwards from the Malay Peninsula to Asia Minor we can see the whole story of money from primitive types to modern forms.

MALAYA AND SIAM

Tin is so abundant in parts of the Malay Peninsula, so easily dug and worked, and so useful for tools, implements and ornaments, that it early took the place of money for local barter and for external trade. It was washed and melted and cast into blocks of certain weights and various shapes, commonly in sugar-loaves, later hollowed into "hats" (*36*), which can be nested conveniently

36. Hat money.

one inside the other. Had these awkwardly shaped "hats" been flattened and made into coins we might have seen the complete evolution from lumps of metal to modern coinage in this region, but, though the "hats" were not withdrawn from circulation until 1893, imported coins, starting with Spanish dollars and Indian rupees and the ever popular Maria Theresa dollars, had long been in general use.

Siam was a little more successful than Malaya in evolving an unbroken series of native money.

A silver coinage may have been in existence as early as the eleventh century A.D., taking different shapes in different parts of Siam. We have "canoes" (*26*) in one district, "shell" or "leaf" coins in

37. Bullets.

another, and the most familiar and most general form the *ticals* or *bahts* which we call "bullets" (*37*). These were simply made. A man melted down the silver into small almond-shaped bars. He nicked one of these across the middle, and hammered it first at one end, then at the other, into a bullet-shaped lump. This was afterwards officially stamped with various marks. The *tical* was worth much the same as the Indian rupee, and there were half, quarter and eighth *ticals* of smaller and smaller sizes. Larger sizes were occasionally minted. An 80 *tical* piece, weighing 39 oz. and about the size of a man's fist is claimed as the largest silver "coin" in the world.

"Bullets" were made in gold, silver and mixtures of tin and copper, and formed the currency down to 1862. In that year King Rama IV, who was anxious to encourage cultural and trading relations with the outside world and especially with Great Britain, issued flat coins in the conventional pattern, and "bullets" fell into disuse, except as buttons.

CHINA

In China we can see the whole story of money starting from the earliest times. Payments were first made in grain, salt or silk, tortoise shells and cowry shells. Then come the entertaining "tool currencies", not only the spades, hoes and knives (p. 18), but also bridge, bell and enigmatic "key" (also called "lily-root") coins, with ring money in bronze perhaps preceded by stone and jade. Finally, the all-conquering *cash* (*40-2*), possibly the earliest coins in the world, as some authorities date them from about 1,000 B.C.

The tracing of the story would be easy if only the Chinese had used a system of dating or if their early historians were more trustworthy in their dates. Historical records written before the Christian era give lists of the forms of money used a thousand or even two thousand years earlier. These include yellow, white and red metal (presumably gold, silver and copper) spades, knives, tortoise shells and cowries. They tell also how the founder of the Shang dynasty in the eighteenth century B.C. issued the first coins at a time when there was a grievous famine in the land, partly to enable the people to buy food, partly that they might redeem the children that they had pawned in their distress. Much the same story of the origin of money is told about Yü, the founder of the Hsia dynasty some centuries earlier. None of the early coins has any inscription, and when inscriptions begin, a few centuries B.C., they can seldom be interpreted with any certainty. They may mark the value or the weight of the coin, or its place of origin, but give no clue to its date. They can be placed in the time of the Chou dynasty, which lasted from 1122 to 249 B.C., but there are no portraits of emperors or other help to their date of issue. The Chinese Empire was at that time less an empire than a loose confederation of states more or less acknowledging the Emperor as their divine head, but mostly warring against each other, each ruling independently, and each making its own form of money. A strong Emperor could enforce currency laws, but these often only added to the general confusion.

GRAIN, SALT, SILK

In the earliest times of which there is any record, grain and salt here as elsewhere took the place of money, and they are often mentioned in early annals, especially as tribute and taxes. Marco Polo describes the salt cakes still used as money in the thirteenth century A.D., stamped with the stamp of the Great Khan and worth about 2d. a cake. Salt cakes are still used as payments for carriers in the hilly regions of Yunnan far from the coast.

China had one other local product, in its silk, that was used as money before coins were in general use, and sometimes after. The Chinese silk industry is traditionally dated as flourishing more than 4,000 years ago and the monopoly was carefully guarded. So silk had a fantastic value and it was literally worth its weight in gold by the time it reached Rome in the early centuries of our era. But in the middle of the sixth century Persian monks sent from Rome hid some silkworm eggs in a bamboo cane and so smuggled them out of China, the monopoly was broken and silk fell in value.

TEA

Tea is another special product of China, used in place of money. It is made up into cakes, stamped with an official stamp and this "brick tea" is still useful in out-of-the-way parts, where coins are seldom seen. The leaves and twigs are collected, dried, beaten, sifted, steamed, fermented and pressed in moulds into flat cakes, or bricks, and then stamped

38. Brick tea (about 1 foot × 9 inches).

and valued according to the weight and quality (*38*). An average brick of some 2½ lb. is worth about a rupee and this is used for paying wages, for buying provisions and in ordinary trading. When Peter Fleming and Ella Maillart were adventuring from China to India in 1935 they carried no money with them, for coins are dangerous possessions in a lawless land. They paid wages and bought camels and food for the journey with brick tea and cloth, welcomed everywhere by people who have no use for dollars.

Grain and salt, silk and tea were used in place of money not only before the invention of coins in China but long after. For coins were so often debased and forged that traders preferred a return to the earlier stage of barter.

COWRIES, INGOTS, CASH

For this reason cowries had a longer life in China than elsewhere. They may have been the earliest, they were certainly the most convenient form of money and were in use for hundreds if not thousands of years. Just as the Latin or Gothic words for cattle enter into the English words "chattels" and "capital", or into "fee" and "fellow", so the word for cowry, *pei*, enters into Chinese signs for precious and valuable, for riches and for money. Heaps of cowries, presumed to have been hoards of money, have been found in prehistoric sites and they are often mentioned in early records. They were officially abolished as currency three centuries B.C., but revived to be officially abolished again some centuries later. Taxes continued to be paid in cowries as late as the fourteenth century A.D., and, as in India, they could have been found until lately in remote parts of the country serving as small change.

Grain, silk, salt, tea and cowries were the money of ordinary people. Gold and silver in lumps or bars were used in more important transactions and for banking, gold from the earliest times and silver from historic times down to the present day. Some of the silver lumps were deeply impressed with a stamp, sometimes

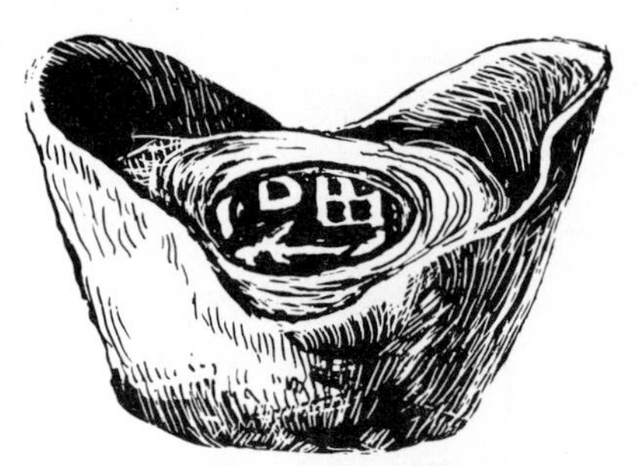

39. Shoe money, China.

with several stamps and from their shape were given their popular name of "shoe money" (*39*). They are more properly called *sycee taels*, the tael being the Chinese *liang*, about an ounce in weight, and *sycee* the name for fine silver. The weights are very variable and scales were needed before the completion of a bargain. Travellers often complained of the time wasted in endless arguments and expressed their relief at reaching a district where coins of fixed weight and value could be used instead.

The continuance of awkward forms of currency in China is surprising when we know that it had a coinage of its own for thousands of years, the typical bronze coins familiar to us as "cash". China can show the longest unbroken series of coins in the world. Possibly we may look for their ancestry to the Stone Age. The stone rings found in prehistoric caves may have served, like the jade and bronze rings of later times, for presents and for tribute if not for trading. According to tradition bronze ring money was accepted for fines some thousand years B.C. Tradition also attributes the earliest bronze coins with a round hole in the centre to the same date. Coins with a square hole in the centre probably date from about 600 B.C. and can claim to have lived with little change through two and a half thousand years. These coins are usually inscribed with value, weight or place of issue, but not with date or any indication of the reigning monarch. As the Emperor was sacred, his portrait or even his name might not be used. It would be desecration for anything bearing his image to be handled by traders.

The earliest coins with the round holes were called *t'ien ch'ien* (*4*), or "heavenly coins", as they were believed to have fallen from heaven. The later coins with square holes—"without, round as the heavens; within, square as the earth"—

40. Pao huo.

41. Pan liang.

42. Wu shu.

are *pao huo*, "valuable exchange", *pan liang* ($\frac{1}{2}$ oz.), or *wu shu* denoting their weight (1 shu = 20 grains of corn), but we usually call them all *cash*, from the Indian name given them by Portuguese traders (*40-42*).

FORGERY

The story of money in China is continually haunted by forgers. The coins were almost invariably in bronze, a mixture of copper and other metals, seldom of silver and more rarely still of gold, and they were cast in a mould, not struck. This made forgery a simple matter and made all coins suspect, thus, as we have seen, prolonging the life of such safer substitutes as grain, silk and tea or the cowries that defied imitation. Another result was the bewildering variety of new coins issued to outwit the forgers. As each emperor, each state, and each important town issued its own coins, the varieties of cash may be reckoned in thousands. Bribes were offered for the detection of forgers, and they were punished with brandings, imprisonment and death. Nevertheless an official complains (about 40 B.C.) that a hundred thousand forgers were discovered in one year.

Tradition, as seen above, dates the earliest Chinese coins about a thousand years B.C., and if this could be proved, China could claim to have invented coins long before the Greeks. Certainly there is no clear evidence of Greek models in Chinese cash and the claim is a strong one, but it must await proof.

INDIA

India also can claim to have invented coins long before the Greeks, but here again, the evidence is uncertain and the dating disputed.

Our knowledge of the earliest history of India has been enlarged in recent years by the remarkable discoveries in the valley of the Indus. Here, in an area rather larger than the British Isles, were found remains of an advanced civilisation more than 5,000 years old. Large merchant cities were laid out on a rectangular plan, with wide streets and well-built houses, fitted with bathrooms and with rubbish shoots. The jade imported from China and Burma in the east and certain seals from Mesopotamia in the west give proof of the extent of the trade, and the decimal measurements and system of weights mark its high standard, but though bronze tools and silver jewellery show fine workmanship there has as yet been no discovery of any form of money. Cowries had not yet reached the Indus Valley, for only a few have been found and they were not money cowries.

This absence of money in a trading centre is so unexpected that certain rectangular and rounded pieces of copper or of silver stamped with various signs have been claimed as money used in the third millennium B.C., but their date is uncertain and so is their use. Nothing in the form of native Indian money can be dated with much probability before about the sixth century B.C., when slightly bent stamped silver bars were in use in the north-west, and a little later, under the Mauryan Emperors, square or oblong punch-marked coins are found throughout the country.

In early times in India as over most of the continent of Asia tribute was paid, debts were collected and payments were made in terms of cattle, grain and other goods. The price of a slave girl in the days of Buddha (sixth century A.D.) was four to six cows or six oxen. The average bride-price was a hundred cows and that was the average blood-price where the man had been insulted, wounded or murdered. Though if a man of the Brahman class killed a man of the Warrior class, the fine might rise to 1,000 cows and a bull.

Cowries as we have seen (p. 25) were a form of money in India from early days down to the present time, and they are still officially recognised, taking a humble place with rupees, annas and pice. In the seventeenth century their value was very variable as they travelled inland. Starting at about eighty to the pice (the fourth of an anna) at the coast, they were worth fifty to fifty-five to the pice at Agra. In the eighteenth century, when five or six thousand cowries went to the rupee, the early revenue of Silhet in Bengal Province was paid entirely in cowries. They were sent down the rivers in boats carrying 50-ton loads and huge warehouses were needed to store them. Even in the nineteenth century cowries still entered into commercial transactions. We read of a gentleman at Cuttack (Orissa) who paid for his bungalow in cowries, though it needed sixteen million of them to make up the £400. In the early years of the present century money-changers in Indian bazaars could be seen with large heaps of cowries ready to serve as small change. In markets far from trade routes there were also lumps of iron, copper or mixed metal all used in place of coins.

43. Punch-marked coin, India.

The use of cowries as money is reflected in the earliest coins common to the whole of India, the so-called "punch-marked" coins (*43*), which probably belong to the fourth century B.C. Their native name is *karshapana* which may be translated roughly as "handful of money", the "handful" being eighty cowries, which represented their value. These coins were simply made. A sheet of metal, silver or copper was beaten out and cut into strips or bars, and these were cut up into pieces of even weight but irregular shapes. The weight of the copper pieces was equal to eighty seeds of the black-spotted pea (*rati*, *Abrus precatorius*) or twice that number of barley grains. Punch-marks were added to guarantee the weight and purity of the metal, sometimes singly, sometimes two or three on top of each other, but usually it is possible to see the signs of the six-armed symbol, and of the sun with encircling rays.

The Persian conquest introduced Persian coins, gold staters or darics, and silver sigloi, which were sometimes punch-marked like the native *karshapana*.

When Persia fell before Alexander the Great in the middle of the fourth century B.C. Athenian "owls" (p. 41) were brought in by traders and became very popular. Later, the power of Rome is shown in the Roman coins that flooded the country, and the head of the Emperor Augustus can be seen representing a native Indian prince.

Bactrian, Scythian and Kushan invaders all left their mark on the early coins of India, and each state as it rose to power issued coins in great variety. At first these copied Greek models and bore Greek inscriptions, but the style alters as the centuries pass and the Greek gods and goddesses are replaced by Indian deities.

Kushan coins show the king on one side and have a generous range of divinities, heroes or saints on the other, Greek, Roman, Zoroastrian, Hindu and Buddhist. The typically Indian coins of the Gupta dynasty from A.D. 320 are of fine gold with Sanskrit inscriptions, excellent examples of Hindu art. Their silver coins were copied from Roman *denarii.*

The first steps towards uniformity and modern types come with the Moslem conquerors, from about A.D. 1000, when gold and silver *tankas* (equal in weight to four beans) show the *kalima* or profession of faith on one side and the name of the king, the mint and date on the other. The magnificent gold coins, sometimes round and sometimes square, of the Great Moguls, Akbar (who conquered India in the middle of the sixteenth century) and his son Jahangir, show beautiful workmanship. The Moguls introduced the *rupee* (which means wrought silver) and the *mohur* or "gold rupee" worth fourteen silver rupees. The English and French East India Companies copied native types down to the middle of the nineteenth century (*44, 45*), with the rupee, fluctuating in value, divided into annas and pice.

The making of images was unlawful, so no portraits are seen on Moslem coins. Instead we have valuable historical information with names and dates of kings and names of mints, as well as quotations from the Koran or other inscriptions. The minting of coins was the special privilege of kings, so it was one of the first acts of any usurper to the throne, and when the

44. Indian mohur.

45. Indian rupee.

reigns of the usurpers were brief and inglorious their coins are often the only record of their rise to fame.

PERSIA: LARINS, DARICS AND SIGLOI

In early times the familiar sequence, cattle, cowries, metals, can be seen in Persia. We read in Persian literature, probably dating some few centuries B.C., the following instructions about the payments to a physician: "He shall heal the master of the house for the value of an ox of low value; he shall heal the lord of the borough for the value of an ox of average value; he shall heal the lord of the town for the value of an ox of high value." Women were doctored for appropriate payments in cows, mares or she-camels.

Cowries spread along the trade routes of Persia from India and were in common use. But they had serious rivals in the *larins* (*46*), short lengths of silver bent in two, so called from Lar, an important trading port of the Persian Gulf. The larins are sometimes curved up at the ends and called "fish-hooks". Sometimes they are open at the ends and called "nose-clips". It has been suggested that they were derived from actual fish-hooks used by the fishermen, or from nose-clips used by the divers of the Gulf, but they are probably merely a handy form of metal currency, especially convenient for tucking into turban or waistbelt. Larins were made in India and Ceylon, as well as in Persia and they were popular even when ordinary round coins had come into general use. An English merchant writing in 1584 describes "this strange piece of money, a small silver rod of the greatness of the pen of a goose feather wherewith we use to write" as "the best current money in all the Indies". This persistent popularity of the larins throughout the Indian Ocean is surprising when we remember that rounded coins had been known for two thousand years.

As noted above (p. 28), Persia and Media were among the greatest powers some six centuries B.C., their only formidable rivals being Babylon, under

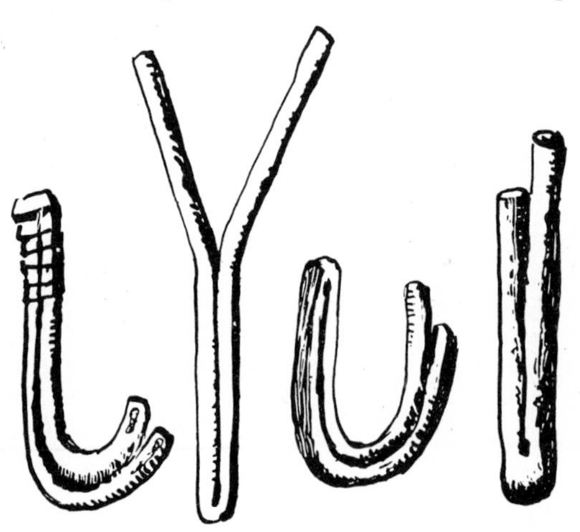

46. Larins.

Belshazzar, and Lydia on the west coast, ruled by Croesus. Cyrus the Great conquered the Medes in 550 B.C., captured Babylon (Belshazzar too late seeing the "writing on the wall", Daniel v) and became "King of the four quarters of the world". He then turned his attention to Lydia where Croesus, then as now, was renowned for his wealth. Croesus was taken prisoner and condemned to be burned, but (according to Herodotus) was miraculously saved when the pyre was already lit, and he lived to be the friend, counsellor and benefactor of the Persian king.

The gold and silver coins of Lydia were already famous in the Eastern Mediterranean and it was on these models that Darius, who conquered his rivals and ascended the throne of Persia shortly after the death of Cyrus, issued his "Persian archers" which were to spread all over the then known world. These

47. Persian daric.

were the gold *darics* (*47*), weighing a little more than a British sovereign, and the silver *sigloi*, weighing a shekel, about equal to an English shilling. The darics were made of the masses of gold dust which (Herodotus tells us) were paid annually in tribute by India. They are roughly oval in shape, having been struck, like those of Croesus, from an egg-shaped globule of gold. On one side we see the king in a kneeling position with a bow in his right hand and a spear in his left. The other side shows merely the rough marks made when the coins were struck. There is no inscription. The king alone could issue gold coins but the satraps, who ruled over allied and conquered provinces were allowed to issue silver sigloi, twenty sigloi weighing twenty shekels being equal to a gold daric.

This proportion of twenty pieces of silver to one of gold is well known to us at the present day, though English shillings are no longer silver and the golden sovereign has been superseded by a paper note.

COINS OF THE HOLY LAND

Silver shekels are familiar to us in the Old Testament. When Abraham bought the field of Machpelah he weighed out 400 shekels of silver "current money with the merchant" (Gen. xxiii, 16). Jeremiah bought land and "weighed money in the balances" (Jer. xxxii, 10). Achan hid his loot of silver shekels under the floor of his tent with disastrous results (Josh. vii, 21). These were all weights of silver, not coins. The first coins to circulate in Palestine were the Persian darics and the Phoenician shekels or tetradrachmas. The Romans introduced their own coins, the best known of which is the *denarius*, commonly translated "penny" in the New Testament, then the daily wage of a labourer. For copper or bronze coins there was the one-tenth of a denarius, commonly translated "farthing", the price of two sparrows (Matt. x, 29) and the still smaller *lepton* or "half-farthing", the "widow's mite" of Mark xii, 42.

The Jews issued their own coins in bronze, but their first silver shekels do not appear until the time of their revolt against Nero in A.D. 66. These coins show "Shekel of Israel" on one side and "Jerusalem the Holy" on the other with types of a chalice and a lily.

COINS OF THE MOSLEMS

As the minting of coins spread throughout western Asia we learn of rulers, some of them otherwise unknown, from portraits or inscriptions on their coins. The fire altar, with or without attendant priests, bears witness to the religion which was dominant for more than a thousand years. A change comes with the invasion of the Moslem hordes of the seventh century A.D. They had no coinages of their own, but when need arose, they adopted types from Byzantine models, *dinars* of gold and *dirhems* of silver. The name *dinar* comes from the Byzantian *denarius aureus* and the name *dirhem* from the drachma.

Towards A.D. 700, with the consolidation of the powers and the increase of riches in the Moslem world, Abd el Malik (687–705) Caliph of Bagdad issued the characteristic coins which were to become some of the most popular and the most wide-spread in European trade from the borders of China to the British Isles.

These handsome dinars were issued throughout the Moslem world from Iran in the east to Spain in the west and it was a dinar of Caliph al Mansur (774) that was copied by Offa, King of Mercia, in England, the Arabic inscription being partly hidden under "Offa Rex".

COINS OF ASIA MINOR

Having briefly traced the story of money and the first beginnings of coins in Asia, travelling from east to west, we reach the western shores and the kingdom of Lydia, where, according to tradition supported by historical evidence, the first coins struck about 700 B.C.

Some three thousand years ago, the traders of Western Asia and round the Mediterranean were using lumps of gold, silver and bronze in exchange for goods, and each was reckoned as the value of an ox. Such were the shekels of Babylonia used by the Phoenicians and the Hebrews of Palestine, and the talents of Greece. But shekels and talents were not coins, they were lumps, bars or rings of certain weights. It may be more than a coincidence that the early bronze talents of Greece were in the shape of a flayed oxhide (*48*) over three feet long or that the figure of an ox was stamped on the rough copper bars of Rome.

48. Bronze "oxhide" ingot, Greece.

"Mankind learnt first to value, then to weigh, and lastly to coin metals." We come now to this last stage in the history of money, the invention of coins in the Eastern Mediterranean about 700 B.C.

It is difficult to decide how much is history and how much is story-telling in the early Greek records, but there seems to be a fair amount of agreement in tracing the earliest coins to Asia Minor. Here, about 700 B.C. Midas was King of Phrygia to the north and Candaules was King of Lydia to the south, while the merchant cities of the coasts and islands were peopled mainly by Ionian Greeks. The Ionians were adventurers, active in industry and in commerce and keen traders by sea and by land. The caravan routes stretching right across Asia brought eastern luxuries to the Mediterranean ports while the good harbours and sheltered, island-studded waters of the Aegean made it easy for the colonists to keep in touch with their motherland. The Lydians, according to Herodotus, were the first shopkeepers. There was one treasure that both Phrygia and Lydia had in common—gold. The legend of Midas is well known, how he was offered a wish and hastily wished that all he touched might be turned into gold. When his food and drink became gold he escaped the threat of starvation by bathing in the river Pactolus, whose sands were thereby turned into gold. The gold was no legend, it was there in abundance, in gold-bearing rocks as well as in sands of rivers such as the Pactolus, which ran through both Phrygian and Lydian territory. The gold was often mixed with silver and it is of this mixture, called *electrum*, and not of pure gold that the earliest coins were made.

PUNCH MARKS

The merchants who used lumps of gold or silver and had to inspect and weigh them for each transaction must often have chafed at the delay. Perhaps some merchant of repute might mark the lumps passing through his hands as a guarantee of weight and purity, for early lumps often show a stamp, such as might have been made by a broken nail, which suggests some such purpose.

TYPES

A mark made by a broken nail might be good enough for a trader, but when the useful invention was taken up by trading ports, by city states, by kings and their officers, they used dies with designs to represent their god or goddess, their royal or civic emblems, to commemorate some local event or to advertise some local product. Thus Lydia shows the royal lion, Phrygia a rosette or a svastika, emblems of the sun, Ephesus had the bee or stag of Artemis, Aegina a turtle and Athens an oil jar, later Athena's owl. When the rulers of the state claimed the sole right of issuing coins, the designs, properly called *types*, became more uniform. Royal names appear on coins, but we have to wait until the time of Alexander the Great before we see the first royal portrait.

The lion and the rosette appear to have been the earliest types on any coins. It may be noted that the lion surmounts the crown on English shillings and the rose forms the centre of the two-shilling piece.

The making of the earliest coins was

at first very simple. All that was needed was a small charcoal-burning furnace, an anvil, a balance for weighing the "blanks" to be made into coins, and a few tools, gravers, punches and hammer, with tongs for holding the molten metal. The metal was placed on the anvil over the die which had the *obverse* design. The punch with the *reverse* design (if any) was placed above, and with a blow struck by the hammer the blob of metal was squeezed into a coin with "head" and "tail".

COINS AND HISTORY

Hitherto we have been tracing the history of money from the earliest times when men lived without any thought or need of it, through their experiments with many forms of primitive money, until by trial and error, it was generally found that metal, weighed and made into coins, was the most satisfactory medium for trading purposes and coins spread throughout the civilised world.

Henceforth coins tell their own story. They can record the rise and fall of kingdoms and of states, the reigns of kings and queens, and their overthrow by usurpers, they tell of victories or defeats by land and sea, of alliances, marriages and murders, in some we can recognise commercial crises, evidence of prosperity or of poverty, the discovery of new mines, their exploitation and their exhaustion. The portraits may not be likenesses, but they are often the only guide to the appearance of the sovereign who issued them and sometimes we can read his character from his profile. Above all, coins reflect the religious beliefs of their day as well as the artistic taste and skill of their makers.

AEGINA AND TURTLES

In the seventh century B.C. the island city of Aegina was the richest trading port of Greece, "the eyesore of the Piraeus" Herodotus called it, when it intercepted the commerce of its neighbours Athens and Corinth. It is related that Pheidon of Argos, whose kingdom included Aegina, struck the first coins, to replace the iron bars or spits that had been formerly used as money. There was no gold in the Peloponnese, but it was rich in iron, so iron bars or spits (*obolos*) were the currency, a handful (*drax*) forming a drachma. Iron money is heavy and cumbersome, as we have seen in modern times in Africa. Plutarch complained that obols to the value of 1,000 drachmas required a large store-room at the house and a yoke of oxen to transport them. The trade of Aegina brought in quantities of silver and it was at a mint at Aegina that Pheidon is said to have coined his silver obols and drachmas which were some 400 times lighter than their iron counterparts.

These earliest silver coins, dating from about 670 B.C., have a leather-backed sea turtle on the obverse (*49*), an emblem appropriate for a sea-faring people, and this was the device of the state for the next two centuries, during which time silver "turtles" (didrachmas, drachmas,

49. Aegina turtle.

50. Amphora, Athens.

half drachmas, obols and half obols) were coined in their thousands and became the staple coinage of the Peloponnese.

ATHENS AND OWLS

At this period Athens was of less importance than Aegina, both in political power and in trading wealth, but she was not dependent on trade for her silver, as she had rich silver mines of her own at Laurium, and she soon (about 610 B.C.) began to imitate the coins of her neighbour. She chose for her didrachmas, drachmas and obols the device of an amphora or jar (*50*), which not only records the importance of pottery as a local industry, but also the profitable export of oil. The olive tree was the valued gift of her patron goddess Athena, and the olive oil of Athens was considered the best in the world.

The amphora continued to be the civic type for many years, while Athens was unified and at peace, but soon different types tell of divisions in the city and the rise of opposing factions, issuing coins with their family badges, such as a wheel, part of a horse, a beetle etc.

Then, about 561 B.C., Pisistratus, leader of the people's party in Attica, seized the Acropolis and became the tyrant and benefactor of Athens, laying the foundations of the city's greatness. By laws within and conquests without, he consolidated the state and he fostered the worship of Athena, his patroness. He issued coins with the head of the goddess on one side and her owl, emblem of wisdom, on the other. As well as the familiar smaller coins he minted tetradrachmas or silver staters, larger and handsomer than the earlier coins, and these are among the first to foreshadow modern types, having devices on both sides (*51*).

Athena's head varies as the years pass, though only in detail. After the Persian defeat at Marathon (490 B.C.) she is crowned with victorious olive-leaves which mark the "owls" of the next two and a half centuries of popularity. Aristophanes in his comedy *The Birds* speaks affectionately of the "little Laureotic owlets — building nests within your purses, hatching little silver pieces", and "to carry owls to Athens" meant in

51. Athenian owl (enlarged).

his time the same as "to carry coals to Newcastle" means in ours.

There was a temporary eclipse about 405 B.C. when, during the wars with Sparta, Athens lost control of the silver mines of Laurium. On her revival the coins were soon reissued with little alteration and on account of their constant weight and good quality silver they retained their popularity not only throughout Greece, but throughout the trading ports of the Mediterranean. Hoards of them have been found in Egypt and Tunisia, as far west as Spain and as far east as India. When most of the city mints were suppressed by Alexander the Great, "owls" were still issued at Athens. The end came only with the end of the supplies. The veins of silver were exhausted and the last "owls" coined about 25 B.C. And so ended the most popular and the longest lived of all the Greek currencies.

CORINTH AND FOALS

Corinth was not long behind Aegina and probably before Athens in setting up its own mint and issuing its own coins, copied from those of Aegina. The device chosen was the winged horse Pegasus, which was especially honoured in Corinth as, according to the legend, it struck the rock with its hoofs, and out gushed the fresh waters of the city. Later Corinth followed Athens in having the head of the goddess Athena on the coins, though she was distinguished from the patroness of Athens by wearing a Corinthian helmet (*52*).

From the seventh century onwards these Corinthian "foals", as they were called, continued with variations for a hundred years and more, and they were imitated by Corinthian colonists to the north as well as by those of Italy and Sicily.

52. Corinthian "foal".

As time went on, all the more important cities and trading ports of Greece and of the Greek colonies round the Mediterranean began to copy this labour-saving aid to commerce, and they issued their own coins with a great variety of types. Some show their city badges, some have heads of gods or of goddesses, some record local legends, or triumphs in the athletic games, some have puns on their names and some show the grapes, fish or grain for which their city was especially famous. But no king or tyrant, however proud or boastful, put his own portrait on any of his coins.

SICILY AND DEMARETE

There was a queen who had a coin named after her and it is not too fanciful to recognise her likeness in the ear-ringed, neckleted lady on the ten-drachma piece issued by Syracuse in 479 B.C. This is a large and handsome coin (*53*). On one side is a four-horse chariot, over it Nike, goddess of victory crowning the charioteer, with an African lion in flight below, thus celebrating the victory of Gelon, Lord of Syracuse, over the Carthaginians. On the other side is the charming head of either the Syracusan goddess Arethusa or Queen Demarete,

53. Demarete, Syracuse.

the wife of Gelon, or perhaps a merging of both, encircled with dolphins. The story goes that after her husband's victory over the Carthaginians Queen Demarete interceded for them in the peace terms, and they, to show their gratitude, presented her with a gold crown and a hundred gold talents. Part she dedicated to the gods, and part was exchanged for silver to make these large coins.

Another famous Syracusan victory coin was struck in memory of the defeat of the Athenians in 413 B.C. showing the conquering chariot and the crowning of the charioteer, with booty spread out below. The beautiful head of the goddess Arethusa surrounded with dolphins appears on the reverse. A still more attractive Arethusa was seen a little later represented full face with dolphins playing hide-and-seek in her ringlets. This coin is signed by Kimon, one of the greatest of the die engravers of ancient Greece. At this period coins attained an excellence which has never been surpassed. There were artists of genius to design them, skilled craftsmen to make them and masses of gold and silver in plenty to provide the material. From the many mints of Italy and Sicily, from those of the mainland of Greece and its islands, from the northern shores of the Aegean and from Asia Minor came coins far more beautiful than any that later centuries could produce.

Meanwhile a power was growing to the north which was destined to sweep away all these local currencies and for the first time to impose a universal type of money over the whole of the then known world.

MACEDONIA AND PHILIPPUS

Macedonia to the north of Greece was regarded as a poor barbarous country with few natural resources. The first step to greatness was taken when, in 356 B.C., King Philip II overran the Ionian cities to the east, conquered the fortress of Amphipolis and possessed himself of the mines of Mount Pangaeus, the richest stores of gold and silver in southern Europe. To guard these treasures he fortified his settlement of Philippi, later familiar to us from St. Paul's epistles to the converts there.

Among the conquered Ionian cities was Olynthus, at whose mint beautiful coins were being made, with the head of Apollo on the obverse and his lyre on the reverse. Philip adopted the head of

54. Stater, Philip of Macedon.

Apollo with his laurel wreath for the obverse of his celebrated gold staters, but on the other side we have a two-horse chariot with his name below, commemorating his successes in the Olympic games (*54*). The "Philippus" as it was called became immensely popular and spread throughout Greece and round the Mediterranean. Hoards have been found in Asia Minor to the east, in Egypt to the south and in Sicily to the west. The coins were carried by trade and later by pillage to France, where they were copied by Celtic tribes, and these were copied again by the Britons. We shall meet them in Kent in the first century B.C., though Apollo and the chariot are hard to recognise.

Philip was a good soldier and a good diplomat and by means of his wealth and his strategy he was able to win over neighbouring states until by 338 B.C. he had conquered the whole of Greece.

ALEXANDER THE GREAT

The conquest of the world was left to Philip's son, Alexander the Great (336–323 B.C.) whose coins were to become international and to continue for centuries. The minting of the popular "Philippi" continued for a score of years after Philip's death, but after a time the staters show a significant change. Alexander was set on the conquest of the great Persian empire and for this he had to have the Greek states solidly behind him, especially Athens with her powerful fleet. So the goddess Athena now appears on the obverse, wearing a Corinthian helmet. The reverse shows Nike, goddess of victory, holding a wreath, and beside her is a ship's standard, emblem of naval power.

Alexander's silver tetradrachmas came to have a wider range and a wider significance. On the obverse is the head of Herakles, whom Alexander claimed as his ancestor. On the reverse is Zeus, greatest of all the Greek gods, seated on a throne with an eagle in his right hand and a sceptre in his left (*55*). The name of Alexander is clearly marked by his side. After he had conquered Persia, his coins spread throughout Asia, and states that knew nothing of Zeus interpreted the enthroned figure as their own local god.

It was Alexander's intention to unite his great empire by the common interests of trade, and a uniform coinage was one of the means to this end. He set up at least a score of mints in various parts, not only in Greece but in Cyprus, Asia Minor, Babylon, Damascus and in Alexandria which was founded and named in his honour. With the wealth of Macedonia as a base and the treasures of conquered cities added, coins were issued

55. Tetradrachma, Alexander the Great.

56. Stater of Lysimachus.

in vast quantities. It has been calculated that some 700,000 silver coins were struck annually at the mint of Amphipolis near the Pangaean mines, for nearly twenty years.

It is interesting to study these silver coins of Alexander the Great, especially the head of Herakles. Herakles (the Hercules of the Romans) was the greatest and most popular of the Greek heroes and the Greeks thought of him as a god as well as a man. Alexander was also thought of as a god as well as a man. When he marched into Egypt and was welcomed by the Egyptians as their deliverer from the Persians, he founded his city of Alexandria and visited the temple of Ammon, the ram-headed god, in the Siwa oasis. Here he was saluted by the priest as Pharaoh, son of Ammon, and given divine honour. It seems as if Herakles with his ram's horns, sign of power and might, becomes merged in Alexander, with the horns of Ammon. After the death of Alexander, one of his trusted generals, Lysimachus, king of Thrace, issued silver tetradrachmas with the portrait of Alexander deified with ram's horns (*56*), one of the earliest and one of the finest portrait heads on any Greek coins. Of special interest is the figure of Athena on the reverse. She is seen seated, her elbow on her shield, with the winged goddess of victory on her extended right arm. This design was copied by the Romans to represent Roma on the imperial coins, and was copied again (p. 62) to represent Britannia on English coppers in the reign of Charles II.

Alexander may be said to bridge the earlier time when only gods and goddesses appeared on coins, and the later stage when the history of a country can be traced in its series of royal portraits. Ptolemy I of Egypt was the first living ruler to set his own portrait on his coins about 300 B.C. In Europe the first representation of a living king is that of Demetrius, King of Macedon (290 B.C.) and this set the fashion which has been followed ever since.

THE SELEUCIDS, BACTRIA AND EGYPT

After the death of Alexander in 328 B.C. his vast and unwieldy empire fell to pieces, and his world-wide coinage, known from India to the shores of western Europe, was succeeded by various types issued by provincial rulers such as the Seleucids to the west, the kings of Bactria and India to the east and the Ptolemies of Egypt. These were turbulent times and governments were weak. Kings were assassinated or ejected by usurpers, themselves to be soon overthrown in turn. Usually the first act of the usurper was to advertise his conquest by issuing coins showing his own portrait and often these are all that we know of his history.

ROME

In Italy and in Sicily, there were colonies of Greeks who had mints and from the fourth century B.C. issued some of the finest coins ever seen.

In strange contrast, the money used by the Romans consisted in rough lumps or bars of bronze, *aes rude*. The unit was the *as* (which may originally have meant a bar) weighing a pound, *libra*, and this was broken up into smaller pieces as

57. Lump of bronze.

needed (57), just as bars of silver were broken up until lately in China. Some of these pieces show signs of having been stamped. Heavy bars weighing five libra are sometimes stamped with the figure of an ox which may have indicated their value.

Soon after 300 B.C. the Romans cast their first heavy bronze coins, *aes grave* (*58*), with heads of gods on one side and the prow of a ship on the other. The head of Janus, god of beginners, is appropriate for their first experiments in coins. The ship's prow represents a victory at sea, for it was the prow of a captured ship that was set up in the Forum as a trophy. These clumsy and cumbersome coins became less clumsy and cumbersome in time, being reduced in weight from a pound to a couple of ounces, and there were smaller fractions. The early types vary little, Janus appearing on the *as*, Saturn or Jupiter on the *semis* or half *as*, Mars or Minerva on the *triens* or third, Hercules on the *quadrans* (fourth), Mercury on the *sextans* (sixth), and Bellona on the *uncia* or twelfth.

The choice of gods or goddesses doubtless had some special meaning, for the Romans under the Republic, and even more under the Emperors, used their coins for advertising and for propaganda. This is especially seen in the constantly varying types of the later silver coins, a hundred variations of which might be

58. Aes grave, Rome.

issued in a year. This gave splendid opportunities for drawing the attention of the public to current events, and many of the figures on the coins may be interpreted as sermons in brief. Thus when civil war threatened, Concordia or Pax would appear on the coins, Libertas when public rights were at stake, while Victoria reminded the people of what they owed to the powers that defended them from enemies or the conquests that spread the glory of Rome. The *victoriate*, so-called from the figure of Victory on its reverse, issued towards the end of the third century B.C., was not for local use, but for foreign trade and advertised the success of the Roman arms.

SILVER

Silver coins were the result of war. Didrachmas were minted in South Italy and more famous coins in Rome itself. According to the story, Rome was in need of money to pay the soldiers in the war against Pyrrhus of Epirus, and asked advice from Juno. Juno promised that money should not fail. When the war ended successfully (269 B.C.) the Romans, in gratitude to the goddess, set up a mint in the Capitol and dedicated it to Juno Moneta, goddess of the mint.

There is probably some truth behind the tradition, but the Roman *denarius*, the best known of all their coins, appears to have been the result of the more famous wars with the Carthaginians, dating from their successful ending about 187 B.C. We see Bellona, the goddess of war, wearing a winged helmet, with "X" inscribed behind her head to show the value of ten asses, and Roma, to guarantee the authority. On the reverse are Castor

59. Denarius, Rome.

and Pollux, the saviours of Rome at the battle of Lake Regillus, riding on galloping horses (59). Of silver also were the *quinarius*, equal to five asses, and the *sestertius*, of two asses, neither of them as popular or as long-lived as the denarius.

GOLD

Gold coins also were the result of war, the earliest being an emergency issue when Rome was engaged in her life and death struggle with Hannibal about 217 B.C. These coins were typically warlike, with the head of Mars, god of war, on one side and the eagle and thunderbolt of Jupiter on the other. But gold coins are rare before the reign of the Emperor Augustus (27 B.C.) whose *aureus* equalled 25 denarii. With the reforms of Nero (A.D. 66), when gold was scarce, the aureus was reduced in weight, and there were thirds, *triens* or *tremissa*. We are reminded of tremissa by the Anglo-Saxon *thrymsa* at the end of the Roman occupation in the fifth century (p. 56).

Constantine the Great, the first Christian emperor (*c.* A.D. 280–337), minted a lighter aureus, called *solidus*, which spread throughout both western and eastern empires, and continued in use almost down to the fall of Constantinople. This splendid series of gold coins, starting before the birth of Christ, showing portraits of successive emperors had no rivals in Europe for some eight centuries. The Arabic *dinars* (p. 38) succeeded them, but the next gold coins to be minted in Europe are the florins of Florence in the thirteenth century (p. 50).

VICTORIATE AND DENARIUS

Gold was rarely used in Italy save by the great ones of the land. It was the silver victoriate and denarius that conquered the markets of the world. The denarius is one of the best known, most widely distributed and longest-lived of Roman coins, as it was minted by the Republic in the second century B.C. and continued unrivalled until the Emperor Caracalla introduced his *antoniani* in A.D. 212. The name survives in the Arabic *dinar*, and the French *denier*, it is reflected in the English penny and finds its way to America where the first Maryland pennies of 1659 are inscribed *Denarius terras mariae.*

In early days it is said to have been the price of a sheep, but it had its ups and downs, mostly downs. In the New Testament it is translated by "penny" as the nearest equivalent to the silver penny, which was the only coin in use in England down to the reign of Edward I. The denarius was the daily wage of a labourer as we learn from the parable of the vineyard (Matt. xx, 2) and it was a denarius with the portrait of Tiberius Caesar with which the Pharisees tried to tempt Jesus in the question of tribute (Matt. xxii, 19). The denarius also enters into our daily life as it provides the d. for the familiar abbreviation of £. s. d. The £ is the *libra*, the weight of the earliest Roman coins (p. 46); the s. is from *solidus*, introduced by the Emperor Constantine the Great in 312; and the d. from the denarius which was known throughout the Roman Empire.

ANTONIANUS

The denarius held its own until the extravagances of the Emperor Caracalla (186–217) and the need to pay his soldiers forced him to take strong action to improve his finances, and he introduced the silver coin probably intended to rank as a double denarius, named after him. Caracalla was only his nickname from the cloak which he wore; his full name was Marcus Aurelius Antoninus, so the new coin was called *antonianus.* At first it was silver, but during the following years (it scarcely survived the century) the silver content became less and less until it was merely copper with a silver wash. In its early years the antoniani show Caracalla as a young and attractive man but after twenty years the features are coarsened and he looks capable of all the murders and cruelties with which he is credited (*60*).

So far the metals used for Roman coins were the familiar ones, gold for the rarely used aureus, silver for the denarius (often

60 a. Caracalla, A.D. 203.

60 b. Caracalla, A.D. 217.

only copper washed with silver) and bronze, i.e., copper mixed with tin, for the *as* and its subdivisions. About the time of Julius Caesar brass, or as the Romans called it *orichalcum*, a mixture of copper with zinc, was imported from Germany or Spain and the *sestertius* and *dupondius*, equal to four and two asses, were henceforth made of the new mixture. The bright yellow coins were attractive and popular and for a time Nero coined the as, semis and quadrans of the same metal.

DIOCLETIAN AND CONSTANTINE

The reforms of the Emperor Diocletian (A.D. 296) and his successor Constantine the Great altered the character of Roman coinage with an issue of uniform coins from the centrally controlled imperial mints, and we hear of new names with new values. The chief gold coin is the *solidus*, with halves and thirds, the chief silver coin the *siliqua* with the double siliqua or *miliarense*, and of bronze or poorer alloys we have the *follis* or double sestertius. These continue until the fall of Rome and pass on to the Byzantine Empire to the east.

PORTRAITS AND HISTORY

Roman coins are remarkable in the stories they tell of the history of their times. Portraits begin in the last century B.C. with Scipio Africanus, the greatest Roman general before Julius Caesar, and Brutus the first consul, founder of the Republic, and others, honoured after their death. The first living man to be seen on a coin is Julius Caesar (44 B.C.) (*61*). Thenceforward portraits prevail and in the time of the emperors from Augustus

61. Denarius, Julius Caesar.

onwards we have a splendid gallery of imperial figures showing us the men who made Roman history. The coins also record the events of their day, such as battles, sieges and victories in wars, with elephant or crocodile referring to conquests in Egypt, and the camel conquests in the East. There are more peaceful scenes celebrating alliances and marriages, athletic games and contests, or distribution of food to the people. We have references to Britain when Claudius shows the triumphal arch set up in his honour after his subjection of eastern England in 46 B.C. or in the picture of the welcome of the pirate emperor Carausius in A.D. 287. Here Britain, represented by a

62. Coin of Carausius.

woman, is grasping the hand of Carausius, exclaiming "Come, O expected one!" (*62*).

BYZANTINE COINAGE

In the fourth century A.D. the power of Rome, which had imposed its coinage on the whole of the civilised world, was declining. First there was the splitting up of the vast sprawling empire, which included Britain with the borders of Asia, into two parts, the Western centred in Rome and the Eastern in Constantinople, where Constantine had founded his city on the site of the former Byzantium. The Western Empire fell before the inroads of the northern invaders. The Byzantine Empire carried on the Roman and Christian traditions until it ended with Constantine XI in 1453.

The chief Byzantine coins are the gold *solidus* or *nomisma*, later familiar as the *bezant* of the Middle Ages. This was divided into *semissis* or half and *tremissis* or third. In the eleventh century the gold coins have a cup-shaped form usually described as "scyphate". Silver was less important and often scarce. The *siliqua* was originally the twenty-fourth of the solidus, and later also becomes cup-shaped, and there was the *miliarense* or double siliqua and *hexagram* or double miliarense. The bronze coins followed the Roman model until the time of the Emperor Anastasius (491–518) whose *follis* is marked with M to signify forty nummia.

The influence of religion on coins is shown in the gradual change from pagan gods and goddesses to Christian signs and virtues. In the early centuries Jupiter the chief god of Rome, with his thunderbolt, sceptre and eagle, or Hercules with his labours, are favourite types, while Mars, god of war, is associated with Rome's many battles, and Juno, queen of heaven, was honoured as Moneta, goddess of the mint. The first signs of Christianity come with the conversion of Constantine the Great, and the cross, the Christian standard or the Christian monogram appear on coins early in the fourth century A.D. The cross becomes a common type henceforward and pagan virtues are easily transformed into Christian virtues. In the turbulent history of Rome, the worship of Victory was universal, and statues to Victory had divine honour. Towards the end of the fourth century, though Victory still appears on the coins, she has become a Christian angel, still with wreath and palm as before but now with the Christian cross.

WESTERN EUROPE

After the fall of Rome the peoples of western Europe began to make their own barbarous coins, at first imitating Greek or Roman models more or less ably. The first great change comes in the eighth century with the reforms of Pepin, King of the Franks (755), and his son the Emperor Charlemagne. Gold was becoming very scarce in the west, while silver was becoming more abundant with the discovery of new veins. Almost the only coins minted in Europe for centuries to come are the silver *deniers*, so-called from the Roman denarius. These usually have a head or bust on one side and decorative crosses on the other. What gold there was came from the east in the Byzantine *solidus* or *bezant*, the most popular coin among European traders, well known as far west as Britain, until supplanted by Edward III's *noble.*

FLORINS AND DUCATS

Gold coins of wide fame were soon to issue from the rich merchant cities of Italy. Florence struck its *florins* and Venice its *ducats* or *sequins* towards the end of the thirteenth century.

63. Florin, Florence.

The florin has the figure of St. John the Baptist on the obverse with the lily of Florence on the reverse (*63*) and takes its name from the flower rather than from the city of its origin.

The *ducat* was so called from a coin first issued by Roger II of Sicily, Duke (*ducatus*) of Apulia, but the gold ducats which were popular throughout Europe came from Venice and are familiar to us from the ducats which Antonio, the merchant of Venice, borrowed from Shylock. They show the figure of Christ on

64. Ducat, Venice.

one side and St. Mark, patron saint of Venice, presenting the standard to the kneeling doge on the other (*64*).

THALERS AND DOLLARS

In the sixteenth century *thalers* were first coined, taking their name from Joachimsthal in Bohemia, famed for its rich silver mines. The large size of these handsome coins gave more scope for the designers and the influence of the Italian portrait medallists (inspired by Pisanello, 1397–1455) stimulated the art of engraving. Thalers became immensely popular and they may be considered the ancestors of all the larger silver coins, the French ecus, English crowns, Italian scudos, and Swedish dalers, as well as the Spanish and Mexican dollars and the dollars of the United States of America.

Germany and Austria had the richest silver mines in the Old World, as Spain had in the New, so thalers and dollars ("pieces of eight", Carolus and Mexican dollars) were issued in vast quantities and became the chief trading coins for the next few centuries. When there was a scarcity of silver at the English mint, they were even adopted as current coin in England, and Spanish dollars of Charles IV were countermarked with the bust of George III, and valued at 4s. 9d., giving rise to the jibe "Two Kings' heads not worth a crown", or the more scurrilous

"The Bank, to make their Spanish
dollars pass
Stamped the head of a fool on the
head of an ass."

Spanish dollars met with a still stranger fate in Australia. The lack of coins there in the early years was a great hardship and the colonists had to make use of whatever foreign types came their way, Spanish dollars foremost among them, and it was difficult to keep these from being sent out of the country. It was a brilliant idea of the Governor in 1813 to make one coin do the work of two for local use only. He had a small circle cut out of the centre, to pass for 1s. 3d., while the outer ring was still valued at 5s. These "holey" or "ring" dollars were withdrawn in 1829.

The thalers of 1780 with the comely bust of Queen Maria Theresa of Austria (*65*) were probably the most popular of

65. Maria Theresa dollar.

all, and these still circulate in the Sudan and along the Red Sea coasts, and in the last century could be met with across North Africa to the Gold Coast. This is surprising, as usually among the less civilised folk the coins of a dead monarch are themselves "dead" and rejected. Maria Theresa died in 1780, but her coins bearing that date were until recently (1950) still minted for East African trade, and accepted as legal currency in Ethiopia.

The history of European money in the Middle Ages is a very complicated one and the coins show a bewildering variety, which is not surprising when kings, princelings, Popes, religious houses, cities and trading guilds all had their own mints, so that we find similar coins called by different names in different countries while unrelated coins often share the same name. Thus for example the ***royal, real, rial*** or ***ryal*** was a gold coin in France in the middle of the fifteenth century and worth about 6s. 8d. In England it was the name of the gold rose noble, which Edward IV raised in value to 10s., though in Scotland later on it was the name of the silver penny. Perhaps it is best remembered in tales of pirates where the silver "pieces of eight" or Spanish dollars worth round about 5s. are so called because they were marked with 8 to represent eight silver reals (*66*).

66. Pillar dollar—"Piece of eight".

OTHER COINS

Since the time of Julius Caesar portraits (in early days better described as caricatures) had been usual on the obverse of coins, with various designs on the reverse, decorated crosses being popular partly on account of their religious meaning, partly, doubtless, because they are easy to draw. *Testons*, *testoons* or *testers* were so called because they showed the *head* of the Duke of Milan (1468) and the name was also given to Italian, French and Dutch coins of the fifteenth and sixteenth centuries. Attempts at representations of the Kings and Queens of England had been made since the time of Offa (p.57), but recognisable portraits are not found before the silver coins of Henry VII; hence these were called testoons. These are the ancestors of our shillings. The device of a shield (Latin *scutum*) gave their names to the French *écu* and the Italian *scudo*, that of a crown (*denier à la couronne* or *écu à la couronne*) in the fourteenth century to the crown piece. When the King of France issued his fine *écu au soleil*, Henry VIII, not to be outdone, issued his "crown of the Rose" in 1526 and the rose has continued to be a favourite design on English coins ever since.

HAMMERED AND MILLED COINS

Down to the sixteenth century, coins were struck by hand on engraved dies and so are called *hammered coins*. But now there comes a change. The Italians invented machines for medal making, used later for coins, by which the metal was rolled out evenly, and discs were punched out and stamped. Because the machines were usually worked by water or horse power the coins were called *mill* or *milled coins*.

It was not long before the rolling mill and the screw press were adopted in the Paris and other continental mints, and attempts were made to introduce them into England in the time of Elizabeth. But these attempts were strongly resisted by the workers at the mint and English coins continued to be made by hand down to the reign of Charles I. Under his patronage, Nicholas Briot, one of the finest die-engravers of Paris, came over to work at the Tower mint and he introduced the new machinery there. With improvements in machines and methods European coins lose their home-made look and become more uniform, not differing greatly in appearance from those issued at the present day.

BEGINNINGS OF MONEY IN BRITAIN

Great Britain, as we should expect, lagged behind the mainland of Europe, as western Europe lagged behind Rome and Greece in the history of money, and the earliest coins made in England are dated about 100 B.C.

Cattle were the chief wealth in Europe, as our words "chattel", "capital", "fee", "fellow", and "pecuniary" all remind us, and although there was no coined money, we have evidence of extensive trade from the earliest times in spite of the isolation of the islands.

In the Bronze Age, Cornish tin and Irish gold attracted traders from overseas and it is possible that beads were used in bartering with the British natives as with African natives centuries later, for Egyptian beads are found in Bronze Age graves in southern England.

67. Gold ring money.

Irish gold comes more clearly into the story of money and it was used by the wealthy instead of coins. Rings were presented as gifts, paid as bride-price and extorted as wergeld or compensation for woundings and killings. They may have been merely ornaments, but when they cannot be worn and are of definite weights they are generally described as ring money. A convenient form was to have a number of smaller rings dangling from a larger one, which may have been worn as a bangle but which could also serve instead of a purse (*67*).

We know a little more about the use of iron or copper bars as money, as Julius Caesar, who invaded Britain in 55 and 54 B.C., gave a description of the island and of the islanders in his Commentaries. Besides mentioning bronze and gold coins he added: "They use . . . iron cuttings, weighed to a definite weight, by way of money." These were the so-called *currency bars* (*68*) found along trading routes or in hoards. They are usually some two feet long and look like unfinished swords and it would be more difficult to accept them as money had we not met the spits of Greece (p. 40) and so many examples of iron bars in Africa (p. 14). Bars of copper probably had the same use in the centuries B.C.

Julius Caesar pictures our ancestors as rude barbarians dressed in skins and stained with woad, but although to the west the tribes were "ignorant of riches other than flocks and herds" (as Mela, the Latin geographer, recorded in the first century A.D.) there were wealthy and powerful kings in the south and east who imported luxuries from France and minted their own coins. Caesar himself told us that they used bronze and gold coins and he extorted large sums of money from them as tribute. It has been suggested that the thousand gold coins found buried in Whaddon Chase were the annual tribute of the Britons on its way to Rome, waylaid, stolen and hidden by the robbers.

EARLY BRITISH COINS

The first gold coins to be found in Britain are those brought over by the Belgae, who landed on the coasts of Kent about 75 B.C. They brought with them gold staters imitated from the popular "philippi" with the head of Apollo on one side, and the two-horse chariot on the other

68. Currency bar.

69. British stater.

(p. 44). But the original can scarcely be recognised. Copiers, and copiers of copiers, have left little of Apollo's head save his wreath, curls and sometimes ears, the chariot has usually disappeared save for an odd wheel, and the horses are curiously dismembered (*69*). None of these Belgic coins has any inscription, so we cannot tell with any certainty when, where or by whom they were made.

The earliest native British coinage is usually called *tin money* and dated between 100 and 75 B.C. Here we have rough imitations of the bronze coins with the head of Apollo on one side and a charging bull on the other that were issued in quantities by the Greek colony of Marseilles, and they were doubtless familiar to the tribes of south-east Britain in their dealings with their kinsmen in France. Britain had been known for centuries as a source of tin and copper from the Cornish mines and it is of a mixture of these metals that these crude pieces are made, cast in a wooden mould. The head of Apollo is little more than a curved outline with a dot for his eye, and the bull is commonly a series of meaningless lines (*70*).

The earliest gold coins made in Britain were, like those brought over by the Belgae, copies of copies of Alexander's staters, and their date is probably about 70 B.C. The head of Apollo can usually be recognised by his wreath and there may be some resemblance to a horse on the reverse, but this often shows nothing but disconnected blobs. Here again there are no helpful inscriptions.

The earliest inscribed coins of Britain are the gold staters found (though very rarely) in Sussex and Berkshire with the name of Commios. There was a Commius, King of the Atrebates, who had territory both in France and in southern England, whom Caesar dispatched (though unsuccessfully) in 55 B.C. to try to win over his neighbouring British chieftains to submit to the Romans. The Commios on the coins is assumed to be his son.

Thenceforward, owing to the influence of the Romans, names of many chiefs and kings are found on British coins, strange names such as Tincommius, Tasciovanus, Dubvellaunus and others unknown to history. The only name of this period which is familiar to all of us is that of Cunobelinus, King of the Catuvellauni, who was Shakespeare's Cymbeline. Cunobelinus reigned over the greater part of south-east England from about A.D. 10 to 40 and he had a mint at Colchester, whose Roman name was Camelodunum. His coins, which are more original than those of his predecessors, have an ear of corn (which may possibly recall Apollo's wreath) with CAMU (short for Camelodunum) on the obverse, and a really

70. British "tin money".

71. Stater, Cunobelinus.

lively horse, often with CUNO, on the reverse (*71*). If there are any heads on any of these early British coins they are the heads of Roman gods or Emperors not portraits of local chiefs or kings.

The Roman conquest brought Roman coins, gold *solidi*, silver *denarii* and *antoniani*, and the commoner bronze and brass. The latter are constantly found scattered along Roman highways, on Roman settlements, or unearthed from hoards which had been buried and never dug up again for hundreds of years. When the Roman legions were withdrawn early in the fifth century, Roman coins were copied for a time in the form of gold thrymsas (tremissa, p. 47), silver *sceats* and copper or brass *minimi*, some no larger than a pin's head, down to the time of Offa, King of the Mercians (757–796). But the copiers transformed Roman heads into birds, birds into roses, wolves into star-fish and star-fish into birds, showing a native delight in animal forms and producing very un-Roman effects.

OFFA AND HIS PENNY

Offa was the first to unify the country and to be called King of the English. He was a contemporary of Charlemagne of France and on friendly terms with him and trade flourished between Britain and the continent. British coins were needed to match the deniers of France, and about 774 Offa minted the English silver pennies which were to be the only coins in use for the next five centuries. These earliest pennies usually have Offa's portrait and his name, sometimes that of his wife Cymethrith, and they show unusual variety in crosses, wreaths, banners, flowers, snakes and other designs, excellent examples of native imagination and native art, far excelling anything to be seen on the continent of Europe at that time (*72*).

When, in the following century, the Danes invaded England, King Ethelred raised large sums for the defence of his kingdom and for bribes to ward off the invaders. The tribute or blackmail was paid in silver and thousands of English pennies were carried off to N.W. Europe and set the fashion in Scandinavia, in Germany and the Netherlands. They were so faithfully copied in Poland that the silver coins of Boleslav the Brave bore the head of Ethelred the Unready of England. These English pennies became as universal and as trustworthy throughout Europe as were the British sovereigns a thousand years later.

The silver penny first minted by Offa in the eighth century continued under successive kings and queens down to the eighteenth century, and it is still struck for the Maundy money which is distributed to poor people at Westminster Abbey every year on the Thursday before Easter. Naturally it has changed in form during its long life of over a thousand years, but from first to last it usually had a head on one side, and various designs, mainly crosses and rosettes on the other.

Immense numbers of these pennies must have been made, as they are often found in hoards of thousands.

72. Offa's penny (enlarged).

When a field was being ploughed up on a farm near Chanctonbury Ring in Sussex in 1866, the plough smashed a pot which had been buried 900 years before, with thousands of silver pennies of Edward the Confessor, and Harold, the last of the Saxon kings. The coins were picked up in hundreds by the workmen and one of them even paid for his pint of beer at the village inn with a dozen of them. About 1700 were collected for the British Museum. This buried treasure is connected in the neighbourhood with the legend of an aged man who used to be seen wandering about the field with his head bent as if looking for something in the ground. A large hoard found in Beaworth, containing over 6,000 pennies, is believed to be one of the gifts that William Rufus sent to the monasteries so that the monks should pray for the soul of his father, William the Conqueror.

HALFPENCE AND FARTHINGS

Although accounts were kept in nominal values of pounds, shillings and marks, no coins other than silver pennies were actually minted from the time of the Norman Conquest down to the reforms of Edward I in the thirteenth century. Halfdene, the Danish king of north-west England, had issued the first halfpennies about 876, and rare round halfpennies are sometimes seen later, but as a rule halfpennies and farthings were simply made by cutting the pennies into halves and quarters.

FORGERY AND CLIPPING

The coins were rude and clumsy and forgery was easy, and the laws show how common it was in spite of penalties of death, or the loss of the right hand. Every local borough could have its local mint and the moneyers were often guilty of issuing coins of debased metal or short weight to make an extra profit. This became such a scandal in the reign of Henry I that it was said that a man with a pound of pennies in his pouch could scarcely get one accepted in the market. Worse still, the soldiers fighting in France complained of the worthlessness of their pay. The King decided that something must be done and he ordered a round-up of all the moneyers in 1125. A chronicler records that almost all were found guilty of fraud and had their right hands struck off.

Clipping was commoner still, and when (down to 1280) the pennies were cut up

73. Short cross penny.

74. Long cross penny.

to make halfpennies and farthings, a little extra clip was simple and profitable. To prevent this, Henry III issued his "long cross" pennies. Henry II had issued "short cross" pennies (*73*), but Henry III had the cross lengthened to reach the edges of the coin, and no coin was legally current unless the ends of the cross could be clearly seen (*74*). In this reign we read "the English penny round and uncut, ought to weigh 32 grains of wheat, taken from the middle of the ear", for the penny was used as a weight as well as a coin, 20 to the ounce and 240 to the pound.

Clipping did not come to an end before the seventeenth century, when coins were machine-made with clear firm edges, thus (as it was said) "saving the life of many a criminal" by removing his chance of a crime. The rims of the thicker coins were stamped with the words *Decus et tutamen*—"ornament and safeguard". Smaller ones had the ridged edge often called "milling" or, more correctly, "graining".

GROATS AND THREEPENNY BITS

In 1279 the silver penny ceased to be the sole currency when Edward I, who struck silver halfpennies and farthings, struck also larger coins, worth four pennies called groats (from the *denarius grossus* of Italy, which also gave its name to the *groschen* of Germany). Groats continued in use, and were joined by the more popular sixpenny and less popular threepenny bits in the reign of Elizabeth. Elizabeth issued quantities of small silver coins. As well as pennies and halfpennies there were for a time threehalfpenny bits, called *dandiprats*, and three-farthing bits. Threepenny bits soon dropped out and during the eighteenth and early nineteenth centuries there was nothing between 6d. and 1d. To fill the gap Joseph Hume, member of Parliament in 1836, proposed the revival of the groat, its special recommendation being that 4d. was the recognised cab fare for half a mile in London. The coins were unpopular with the cabmen and derided under the name of "Joeys" and ceased to be coined, save as Maundy money, in 1856.

Silver threepenny bits issued in 1839 continued until superseded by the twelve-sided aluminium-bronze "thrift" coins of the present day. The first of these were among the rare coins with the head of Edward VIII, issued in 1936.

FLORINS, NOBLES AND ANGELS

No gold coins were struck in England between the reigns of William I and Edward III, save the gold penny of Henry III, with the figure of the king enthroned on one side and the long cross with roses on the other. This does not seem to have been popular. In the prosperous reign of Edward III, when the country was free from civil wars, the lack of gold was a serious matter and a petition was sent to Parliament calling for a remedy. We saw (p. 50) that the gold florin was one of the most popular coins of Europe when the bankers of Florence were the bankers of Christendom, so two Florentine goldsmiths were invited over to England to make the first florins in 1344, but these had only a short success, being supplanted in the same year by the famous Edward III *noble*.

The florin comes into the story of English money again when, in response to a demand for a decimal coinage in 1849, the two-shilling piece, called also *centum*, *decade* and *dime*, was introduced to represent the tenth of the pound. The first issue raised a storm of protest as the letters D.G., for *Dei gratia*, "by the grace of God", had been omitted. They were called "godless" or "graceless" florins. The letters were restored in later issues, as can be seen on the two-shilling pieces, still called florins, of the present day.

Edward III's noble is believed to commemorate the Battle of Sluys in 1340 when the king defeated the French fleet and gained command of the seas—

"Four things our noble shows to me
King, sword and ship and power of the sea."

75. Noble (enlarged).

The coin, worth 6s. 8d. shows the king (enlarged) on a ship, and this continued as the popular type for more than a century (*75*).

In the reign of Edward IV a rose was added to the ship and the coin was called the *ryal* or *rose noble* and its value raised to ten shillings (*76*).

76. Rose noble (enlarged).

A coin worth 6s. 8d. (the standard professional fee) was needed, and the need was supplied by the famous *angel*, so-called from its design of St. Michael killing the dragon. This may have had reference to the victory of York over Lancaster after the Wars of the Roses, but was popularly accepted as the victory of good over evil and it was this coin (later a medal with a similar design) which was used by the kings and queens of England from Edward down to Queen Anne, for "touching for the King's evil" as a cure for scrofula. On the reverse, the ship still rides the waves, but the figure of the king has gone and his shield supports a cross.

PORTRAIT HEADS

Down to the time of Henry VII the coinage was mainly conventional, with gold nobles and angels, silver groats, half groats, pennies and halfpennies, bearing the figure or head of the king, but with little attempt at a likeness. Henry VII issued new coins with new designs and they are distinguished by being the first to show, in place of the conventional heads, a dignified profile portrait. This was the work of the German engraver Alexander, from Baden. Henceforward we have an unbroken series of royal portraits of all the kings and queens of England, though few of them are so much admired as that of Henry VII.

The special new coins of Henry VII were the sovereign, worth 240 pence, which continued with variations down to the present century, and the testoon worth twelve pence which in the next reign was also called a shilling. Shakespeare's characters speak sometimes of "testers" sometimes of shillings, and this appears to have been the price of admission to the theatre in his day.

77. *Angel (enlarged).*

THE ENGLISH SOVEREIGN

The English sovereign which succeeded the Spanish or Mexican dollar in the trade of the world had very varied fortunes and very varied names. It was first called a sovereign in 1489, in the reign of Henry VII. In the reign of James I of England and VI of Scotland it was called the *unite*, from the surrounding legends such as *Henricus rosas, regna Jacobus*, "Henry (united) the roses, James the kingdoms", and *Faciam eos in gentem unam*, "I shall make them one people". It was popularly called a *broad* as it was beaten out very thin and wide, nearly $1\frac{1}{2}$ inches across, or a *laurel* or a *sceptre* from its designs. In Charles II's time it gained the name of *guinea* because the gold came from the Guinea coast of Africa. It had its ups and downs in value, sometimes as high as 30s., sometimes as low as 10s.

After the gold standard was fixed in 1816 the new sovereigns were issued with the fine design by Pistrucci of St. George and the dragon, which shows up well on the crown piece (*78*). St. George was chosen in compliment to King George III, but the model is said to have been a waiter at Pistrucci's hotel in Leicester Square.

78. St. George.

Being "worth its weight in gold" the sovereign was especially valued in time of financial disturbance. Most of the continental countries had adopted paper money as early as the eighteenth century, but this was often suspect and in time of war or commerical crisis could vary from week to week, sometimes from hour to hour. Sovereigns are still hoarded in Greece. It was calculated (in 1954) that 15 million were in existence though not in circulation, one being worth 85,000 drachmas. Here Queen Victoria meets with less respect than Queen Maria Theresa of Austria (p. 52) for, according to well recognised trading rules, the ratio of "male" to "female" sovereigns must be 4 to 1, one Queen Victoria (*85*) being balanced by four Edwards or Georges.

The Great War of 1914–18 ended the reign of the golden sovereign which had lasted for over 400 years, and its place was taken by Treasury notes, familiarly called "Bradburies" from the signature of the Chief Clerk at the time. Since 1928 notes have been issued by the Bank of England.

HALFPENNIES AND FARTHINGS

During the sixteenth and seventeenth centuries English coinage was in confusion and the lack of small change led to the issue of traders' tokens for local use. The silver for the testoons or shillings (first coined in 1548) and the half shillings or sixpences (first coined in 1551) was constantly being debased with alloys, and it must have been difficult and risky for traders when these coins were being issued at different values and in differing weights at different mints, or even from the same mint. No wonder that they preferred their own tokens which they (and their customers) could recognise. There were grave scandals which added to the confusion, as when Sharington, in charge of the Bristol mint, confessed in 1548 to having issued thousands of pounds-worth of coins, counterfeit, under-sized and under-weight, to have falsified books and burnt documents. He escaped with a fine and imprisonment for a few months in the Tower.

It was Charles II who introduced copper halfpennies and farthings in 1672 to provide small change in place of the tradesmen's tokens which were no profit to the Crown and, though usually illegal, were made on an enormous scale.

The King Charles II halfpenny (79) is noteworthy for the figure of Britannia,

79 a. Halfpenny of Charles II, reverse.

the forerunner of the Britannia on modern pennies. The Duchess of Richmond, the celebrated beauty of the court, was popularly believed to have sat as the model, but the original was the figure of Roma on the sestertius of the second century A.D., itself copied from Athena on the coins of Thrace about 300 B.C. (p. 45).

King Charles's coins are noteworthy for another characteristic. When not posing as a Roman Emperor, wearing a wreath, they show him wearing a crown, but the crown does not appear on the head of a monarch again until we see it

79 b. Halfpenny of Charles II, obverse (enlarged).

on the head of Queen Victoria in 1847.

The Queen Anne farthings (*80*) may be mentioned here as no farthings have

80. Farthing of Queen Anne, obverse (enlarged).

ever attained so remarkable a notoriety. The rumour went about that only three had been coined before the die was broken up, so a fictitious value was put on them and £50 or even £200 are said to have been paid for a single farthing. In 1818 an unfortunate man was accused of having borrowed and not repaid one of these farthings and he was sentenced to a year in prison.

PENNIES

Silver pennies were still issued during the seventeenth and eighteenth centuries, but with the growing scarcity of silver they were no longer plentiful and in 1730

81. Cartwheel penny, George III.

they ceased to be coined, save for Maundy money.

In 1797 some clumsy heavy copper pennies were issued, called "cartwheels" (*81*) to be followed in 1860 by the bronze Victorian coins with which we are all familiar. Indeed so long-lived are they that pennies with the date of 1860 still clearly to be seen are not uncommon today. The pattern penny for this new series came to an ignominious end. It was sent to Queen Victoria for approval and she returned it by registered post. The postman, yielding to temptation, took it to a secluded place and broke open the packet. He was so disgusted to find only a penny inside that he threw it down a drain, and it was lost for ever.

Some pennies have, like Queen Anne farthings, attained fictitious values. Pennies were issued in an unbroken series from 1860 to 1922, but owing to world upheavals there are none for 1923, 1924 and 1925, nor for 1941, 1942 and 1943. In 1933 the mint struck six pennies for special purposes and it is popularly believed that one of these is in circulation and worth a fabulous sum. People are often deceived also by the statement that 1920 pennies are worth £8. A little calculation will show that as 240 pennies go to the pound, the statement, though deceptive, is literally true.

The English penny may claim an almost unbroken life of nearly a thousand years, with a more stable history than that of any other coin. There were 240 to the pound in the time of King Offa, and there are 240 to the pound now. Perhaps this very fact may have been the chief obstacle to the attempt, so often proposed, to introduce decimal coinage into Great Britain. The Royal Commission appointed to examine the proposal in 1920 considered an attractive and logical scheme, dividing the pound into 1,000 mils. But when it was seen that this would mean the disappearance of the penny it had little support.

Our pennies reflect times of prosperity and times of scarcity, royal pride and royal debasement, wars abroad and civil wars at home. They give us records, if not portraits, of all the kings and queens from Offa to the present time (with a kingless interval for the brief Commonwealth, 1649–60), and they illustrate the artistic skill of their day.

Gone are the Athenian "owls", gone are the golden "philippi", gone are also our own golden sovereigns, but the British penny, though altered in appearance, is still our most familiar coin. Its popularity and its common use are shown in our many sayings, such as, "Penny wise, pound foolish", "In for a penny, in for a pound", or, "to turn an honest penny", where penny means almost the same as money.

MONEY IN THE AMERICAN COLONIES

Before the Spanish, Portuguese, Dutch, French, British and other adventurers brought their coined money into the New World in the sixteenth and seventeenth centuries, the native Indians traded mostly by barter and there was very little that could be called local money. There were shell beads or strings on the coasts of which the most important and widely spread was *wampum* (p. 23), though it was valued chiefly as ornament and used more for presentation than for trading. The *coppers* of the North West coast (p. 7) were also more for ostentation than used as money.

The early colonists from Britain who went out to seek their fortunes in the unknown continent took little money with them and the shortage of coins, especially of small change, was a constant complaint. The colonists made use of wampum on the mainland, and it was officially recognised as legal tender in Massachusetts in 1643 at six or eight beads to the penny. But the factory-made strings of the eighteenth century were turned out in such quantities that it soon became almost worthless as currency. For the most part, the colonists were reduced to barter, exchanging tobacco, corn, sugar, rum, cotton, timber, molasses, ginger, indigo and skins. The smallest coins in general use were the Spanish reals, worth about 6d., and the lack of anything smaller (as a writer to the Treasury complained in 1701) "puts the inhabitants to the necessity of carrying sugar and tobacco upon their backs to barter for little common necessities". This was however something more than merely barter, as the colonists attempted to fix the value of these goods so that they could take the place of money.

In Virginia the General Assembly fixed the price of tobacco in 1619, and indeed passed a law a few years later, making it the sole currency. But as anyone could grow tobacco and it grew freely, it flooded the market and the price could not be maintained when its actual value was only 2 cents a pound.

In Maryland in 1708, tobacco is described as being "meat, drink, clothing and money", the usual standard of trade and means of exchange with planters as with merchants and the price was fixed by law. In Virginia also, tobacco was the current money, and when in the seventeenth century "young and uncorrupt girls" were imported as wives for the settlers, a writer says "it would have done a man's heart good to see the gallant young Virginians hastening to the waterside when a vessel arrived from London, each carrying a bundle of the best tobacco under his arm and taking back with him a beautiful and virtuous young wife". The "bride-price" was 100 lb. of tobacco, valued at £15.

Brown sugar was legal tender in Barbados, rated at 10s. per 100 lb. and the merchants complained, in 1664, that the islanders had no money except sugar. Fines were paid in sugar, the penalty for cursing or swearing was 4 lb. of sugar if a master or a freeman, and 2 lb. if a servant. Colonial Acts levied taxes, prescribed fees, and imposed fines in sugar. An "able preaching minister" was paid 14,000 lb. of sugar a year in the Leeward Islands and he could charge 100 lb. for a marriage service. Land was bought and sold for sugar (at 1,000 lb. an acre) and fees were paid in sugar as late as 1735.

Furs and grain were legal currency in Canada, wheat at 4 francs for 3 bushels and beaver skins at market prices. *Card money*, stamped with the *fleur de lis* and a crown, was issued from 1685 onwards, with disastrous results, and for nearly a century the colony "floundered in drifts of worthless paper". The British in 1764 attempted to fix the relative values of the moidores and "Joes", thalers and louis d'ors, pistoles and guineas, Spanish dollars, French crowns, English shillings and sixpences which jostled each other throughout the country, but coins were always scarce and often clipped and debased.

Appeals to the Treasury were constantly being made by the colonists on the mainland of America as well as from the West Indies, asking for supplies of coins, but the Treasury had its own troubles at home (p. 61) and English coins could do little to establish currencies abroad. For the gold coins the colonists had to put up with Spanish doubloons and pistoles or Portuguese moidores and Johannes, familiarly called "Joes", and other foreign coins.

AMERICAN MINTS

The colonists had already been making attempts to set up their own mints and to make their own coins. One of the earliest efforts was that of John Hull of Boston, who issued coins without royal licence but with the authority of the General Court of Massachusetts in 1652. These coins were shillings, sixpences and threepennies with various devices of which the best known are the willow, the oak tree and the pine tree. A little later (1659) Lord Baltimore of Maryland had shillings and sixpences, groats and copper coins minted in London and exported to his colony.

CENTS AND DIMES

During the eighteenth century, many of the American States issued their own coins or tokens, beginning with shillings and pence. Vermont and Connecticut were the first to coin copper *cents* in 1785 and half dollars are among the Washington pieces issued in 1793. The Mint Act of 1792 authorised the setting up of a mint in Philadelphia, striking *dimes* (from *decimus*, the tenth of a dollar) and half dimes, with the head of Liberty on one side and the American eagle on the other. Scrap metal was collected throughout the States and melted down. Washington himself is believed to have contributed "an excellent copper tea kettle and two pair of tongs" to make the cents of 1793.

These early cents, "old coppers" as their collectors affectionately call them, show great variety, starting with the chain, wreath and Liberty cap, and more than 300 types were issued in the next twenty years, though many are so scarce as only

82. Five cents, U.S.A.

to be seen in museums. In 1815, wars with England stopped supplies of metal and the early issue ceases. Variations have continued down to modern times with the popular buffalo and Indian chief (*82*).

The first mint in Philadelphia was a very modest establishment with poorly paid workers. Horses were used for the heavy rollers, but as most of the work was done by hand, irregularities give individuality to the coins which were not appreciated then as they are now. Congress disapproved of the mint, which was run at a loss, and frequently introduced bills for its closure. The public made fun of the cents, calling the eagle a sick turkey-cock and Liberty a wild squaw. After 1815 the mint began to prosper with new buildings and new machinery, and when a new mint was opened in 1833 the machine-made coins become of less individual interest.

THE DOLLAR

Gold was rare in the United States; the coins in general use were the silver pesos, piastres or "pieces of eight" (p. 52) later called *dollars*, as they were roughly equivalent in value to the thaler, at about 5s. These were the coins which dominated the trading world for three centuries in Europe, America and the West Indies, and also round the coasts of Africa, in the Malay Peninsula (where they are still current) and in Australia.

It is interesting to notice the alteration in these dollars after the discovery of the rich silver mines of Potosi in 1545. The Pillars of Hercules, which earned for them the name of "pillar dollars", had the motto *non plus ultra* "no more beyond", founded on the belief that they were the end of the world. After the voyages of Columbus and the Spanish conquests of Mexico and Peru had opened up the dazzling riches of the New World the motto becomes *plus ultra* to commemorate discoveries of lands of which Hercules had never dreamed. The upright lines of the dollar sign, $, may be derived from the Pillars of Hercules, but the device is usually attributed to the Spanish contraction for *peso*, a weight. Spanish and Mexican dollars held their own until revolts in Spanish-America cut off supplies early in the nineteenth century.

Henceforward, the United States dollar is the dominant coin. It shows on one side the head of Liberty, the symbol of independence, with thirteen stars to represent the thirteen original states of the Union (*84*). On the other side is the American eagle with outstretched wings. On the "Peace dollar" of 1921 the eagle has folded its wings.

83. Quarter dollar, U.S.A.

84. Dollar, U.S.A.; "Peace dollar" on right.

Though silver dollars have dropped out of use, being replaced by paper notes, it is dollars that dominate the world to-day and are the last word in the story of money. There are some who believe that before long coins will be a curiosity of the past and that dollar paper notes with their subdivisions will form the currency of the world.

PAPER MONEY

Paper money is usually regarded as a modern invention, and older people of the present generation in England can remember when paper notes were rarely seen. But if we take I O U s or promises to pay as their origin, we have to go back to the beginnings of history. More than seven centuries B.C., merchants in Assyria gave promissory notes and used bills of exchange. These were of course not paper, but were records stamped on clay, promising to pay certain weights in silver or in copper. Such clay tablets can be seen in the British Museum so well preserved that they are almost as clear today as when they were first issued.

As there were no banks, rich people stored their wealth where they could—in temples, as in Egypt and in Babylon, with the rich merchants, the money-changers or money-lenders, in the vaults of jewellers or goldsmiths or in the safe keeping of monasteries. From all these stores money could be drawn by the owner when needed by a form of cheque.

As commerce expanded, credits became more and more necessary and private bankers more and more unsatisfactory. Barcelona claims the oldest city bank, founded in 1401, with Genoa a little later. Venice and Milan followed in the sixteenth century, Hamburg in 1619, with the Bank of England, the first national bank issuing its first authorised bank-notes, in 1694.

According to Chinese historians, China was the first country to issue bank-notes, and it came about in this way. The Emperor, about 200 B.C., had in his royal park a white stag believed to be the only one in the world. He had it killed and had the skin made into smallish pieces, and gave to each piece the value of 400,000 copper coins. When princes came to pay homage to their Emperor they had to buy one of these "White stag notes" for cash and offer their gifts on it. This ingenious invention was the fore-runner of the paper currency, called "flying notes", recorded in China a thousand years later. Towards the end of the thirteenth century Marco Polo, the Venetian traveller, gave an account of the paper money of Kublai Khan. The sheets of paper were made from the inner bark of the "paper mulberry tree" and stamped with different values varying from half the tenth of a penny up to ten gold bezants. "All these pieces of paper," he says, "are issued with as much solemnity and authority as if they were of pure gold and silver", and with them the Emperor "causes all payments in his own account to be made and he makes them to pass current universally over all his kingdom and provinces and territories and whithersoever his power and sovereignty extends".

In England, after the Conquest, the Jews were the chief bankers and money-lenders, other trades being denied to them, and when they were expelled from the country in 1290 their work was carried on by the Lombards, rich merchant-bankers from Italy, whose name is preserved in Lombard Street in London. Edward I and successive kings depended on loans for financing wars and other state enterprises and the Lombards had immense influence on European politics. For lesser folk the goldsmiths were the usual bankers. They had vaults in which money could be stored and they issued vouchers payable on demand which could be passed from hand to hand. Another place of safe-keeping was the Mint in the Tower of London where merchants deposited their surplus cash. But a shock was awaiting them, for in 1640, King Charles I, being in desperate need of money seized deposits amounting to £120,000, repaid only after violent protests and after a considerable length of time. A further requisition in 1672 brought ruin to goldsmiths and financial chaos to merchants. The need for some safeguard against such accidents was acute and in 1691 the Chancellor of the Exchequer adopted the scheme of William Paterson, and the Bank of England was founded in 1694 in the Grocer's Hall, London, taking up its present position in Threadneedle Street forty years later.

The "Old Lady of Threadneedle Street" was accepted as a national character and "safe as the Bank of England" became a common saying.

Paper notes have often been used as emergency money in time of war or other crisis in many parts of the world. "Card money" was the ingenious expedient of the Governor of Canada when (in 1685) the troops were on the verge of mutiny with pay long overdue. He collected playing cards, had them stamped with different values and added his own signature. But when the government proceeded to issue "card money" in large quantities, and when it was forged in larger quantities still, public confidence was shaken and it came to an end, though most of the colonies issued their own paper money down to the time of the Revolution. *Greenbacks*, the U.S. issue of 1862, were so called because the devices on the back were printed in green ink, and their descendants, *bucks*, may prove to be the last stage in the story of money.

85. Sovereign.

A SELECT BOOK LIST

REVISED BY NORMAN STONE, A.L.A.

ANGELL, NORMAN. *The Story of Money*. Cassell, 1930. Illus., book list. For the advanced student.

BROWN, LAURENCE. *Coin Collecting*. Arco (Handybooks Series), 1962. Illus., book list. A simple introduction.

CHAMBERLAIN, C. C. *The Teach Yourself Guide to Numismatics: an A B C of Coins and Coin Collecting*. E.U.P. (Teach Yourself Series), 1960. Illus., book list. A guide arranged as a dictionary.

COPE, A. C. *Money*. E.S.A. Illus., book list. A simple introduction to monetary theory.

HANSON, J. L. *Money*. E.U.P. (Teach Yourself Series), new ed. 1959. Tables, book list.

JOSSETT, C. R. *Money in Britain: a History of the Currencies of the British Isles*. Warne, 1962. Illus. Contains a useful summary of the coins and printed note issues in Great Britain.

LINECAR, H. W. A. *Coins*. Benn, new ed. 1962. Illus., book list. Contains useful appendices.

QUIGGIN, A. H. *A Survey of Primitive money: the Beginnings of Currency*. Methuen, 1949. Illus., maps, book list. A detailed account of the subject, more suitable for the advanced student.

SUTHERLAND, C. H. V. *Art in Coinage: the Aesthetics of Money from Greece to the Present Day*. Batsford, 1955. Illus., book list. A history of art and design in the coinage of the western World.

The articles on "Numismatics" in the *Encyclopaedia Britannica* and *Chamber's Encyclopaedia* will be found useful, and collectors will need to consult Seaby, H. A. *and* P. J. *Standard Catalogue of the Coins of Great Britain and Ireland* (published frequently).

Index

(The numbers in italics refer to illustrations)